Do something today
that your future self
will thank you for.

THIS BOOK INSPIRES ME DAILY

© Turtle Creative | Synk Media

Published by Synk Media

All rights reserved.

Printed on demand in Australia, United States and United Kingdom.

Edited & designed by Turtle Creative.

Uplevel your Life Journal
© Katherine Shanks 2020

All rights reserved. No part of this publication may be reproduced, stored in a retrieval system, or transmitted in any form or by any means, electronic, mechanical, photocopying, recording or otherwise, without prior written permission of the author.

PRINT ISBN 978-0-6488986-0-3

## If you want to uplevel your life, you must uplevel your mindset!

It was these words that stopped me in my tracks at a personal development seminar one day. The more I thought about it, the more I realised that there was so much more to it.

Sure, it's easy to say 'change' your mindset... but HOW? HOW can I completely change the way I think? HOW can I make these changes permanent?

So I started developing habits to make this shift. It took a bit of trial and error, but I developed a simple daily and weekly process that helped me make permanent shifts in my habits and my mindset.

### "If you keep doing what you always did, you'll keep getting what you always got."

It's this quote that inspires me everyday to slightly improve upon the day before.

It's my hope, that this journal will help you create the small shifts that are required to bring about massive change in your life. The aim of this journal is to:

✓ Create a vision for what the future holds
✓ Improve the way you talk to yourself
✓ Focus on the present and the future, not dwell on the past
✓ Commit to habits that align with your future self
✓ Develop daily rituals for your mind, body & soul
✓ Set daily tasks to keep you accountable to your goals

*Kathy* xx

A journal inspired by my family.
Jason, Charlie & Jenna
They are the reason I always
strive to uplevel my life!

# Journal daily to Uplevel

Welcome to the beginning of the new you! This journal is designed to create daily actions EVERYDAY to create the future of dreams.

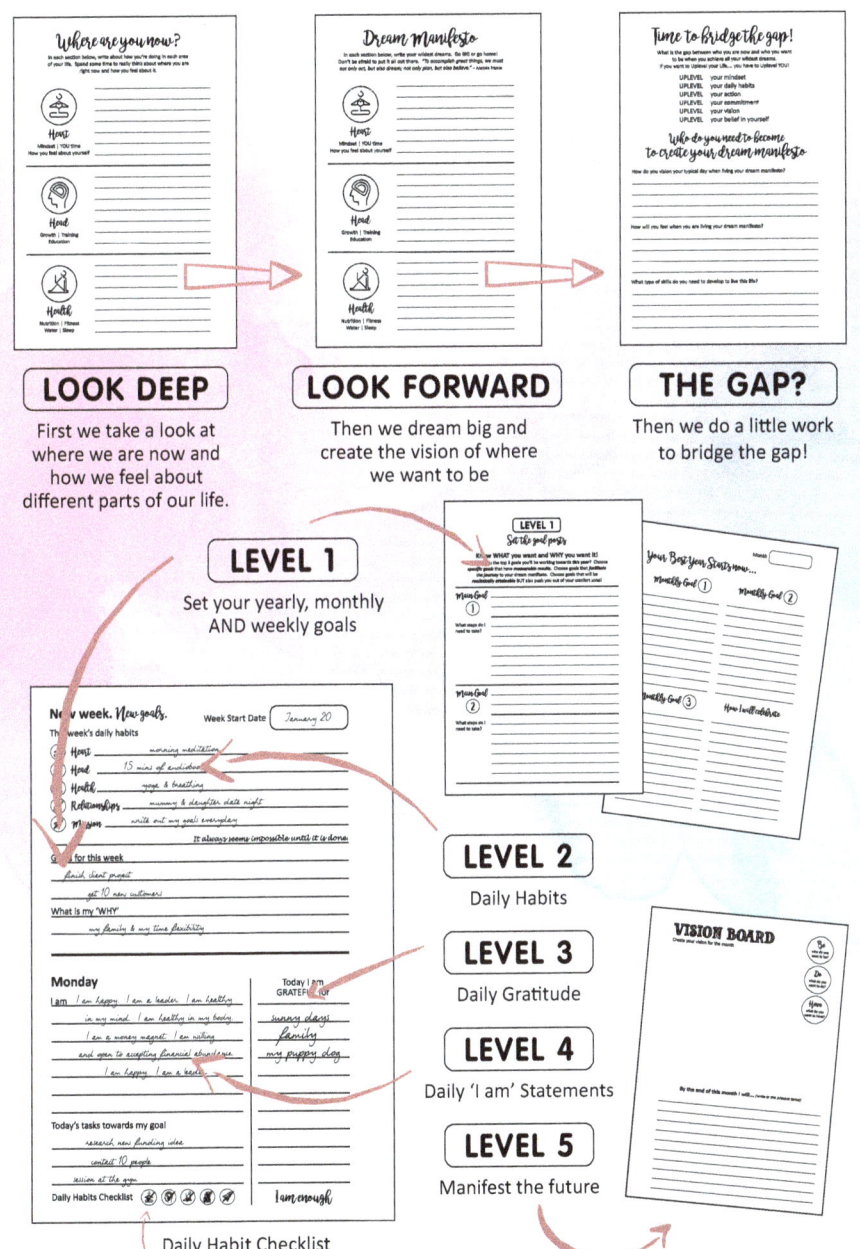

**LOOK DEEP** — First we take a look at where we are now and how we feel about different parts of our life.

**LOOK FORWARD** — Then we dream big and create the vision of where we want to be

**THE GAP?** — Then we do a little work to bridge the gap!

**LEVEL 1** — Set your yearly, monthly AND weekly goals

**LEVEL 2** — Daily Habits

**LEVEL 3** — Daily Gratitude

**LEVEL 4** — Daily 'I am' Statements

**LEVEL 5** — Manifest the future

Daily Habit Checklist

# Where are you now?

In each section below, write about how you're doing in each area of your life. Spend some time to really think about where you are right now and how you feel about it.

## Heart
Mindset | YOU time
How you feel about yourself

_____
_____
_____
_____
_____
_____
_____
_____

## Head
Growth | Training
Education

_____
_____
_____
_____
_____
_____
_____
_____

## Health
Nutrition | Fitness
Water | Sleep

_____
_____
_____
_____
_____
_____
_____
_____

_____
_____
_____
_____
_____
_____
_____
_____

## Relationships
Personal
Family | Friends

_____
_____
_____
_____
_____
_____
_____
_____

## Mission
Career | Finances
Business | Charity

**What do you LIKE about these thoughts?**

_____
_____
_____
_____

**What do you DISLIKE about these thoughts?**

_____
_____
_____
_____

# Dream Manifesto

In each section below, write your wildest dreams. Go BIG or go home! Don't be afraid to put it all out there. *"To accomplish great things, we must not only act, but also dream; not only plan, but also believe."* – Anatole France

## Heart
Mindset | YOU time
How you feel about yourself

_____
_____
_____
_____
_____
_____
_____

## Head
Growth | Training
Education

_____
_____
_____
_____
_____
_____
_____

## Health
Nutrition | Fitness
Water | Sleep

_____
_____
_____
_____
_____
_____
_____

They say I dream too big.
## I say, they think too small.

_____

## Relationships
Personal
Family | Friends

_____

## Mission
Career | Finances
Business | Charity

Take a moment to think about what your life will be like.
How will feel when you reach these goals?

_____

# Time to bridge the gap!

What is the gap between who you are now and who you want to be when you achieve all your wildest dreams.
If you want to Uplevel your Life.... you have to Uplevel YOU!

**UPLEVEL** your mindset
**UPLEVEL** your daily habits
**UPLEVEL** your action
**UPLEVEL** your commitment
**UPLEVEL** your vision
**UPLEVEL** your belief in yourself

## Who do you need to become to create your dream manifesto

How do you vision your typical day when living your dream manifesto?
_____
_____
_____
_____

How will you feel when you are living your dream manifesto?
_____
_____
_____
_____

What type of skills do you need to develop to live this life?
_____
_____
_____
_____

What traits will you have when living your best life?
(for example Confidence, Assertiveness, Credibility, Focused, Compassionate)

___

___

___

___

What limiting beliefs, fears or patterns are holding you back or may limit you from achieving your dream manifesto?

___

___

___

___

**CREATE CERTAINTY IN YOURSELF!**
Remind yourself that you are already amazing! Write down anything in your life that was once just a goal, dream, or desire. Big or little - what are some of the things that at one time seemed extremely difficult or impossible to achieve or acquire? If you ever feel like giving up - come back and read this!

___

___

___

___

___

___

___

___

___

___

# LEVEL 1
## Set the goal posts

**Know WHAT you want and WHY you want it!**

What are you the top 3 goals you'll be working towards *this year*? Choose *specific goals* that have *measurable results*. Choose goals that *facilitate the journey* to your dream manifesto. Choose goals that will be *realistically attainable* BUT also push you out of your comfort zone!

### Main Goal ①

_____
_____
_____

**What steps do I need to take?**

_____
_____
_____
_____
_____
_____
_____
_____

### Main Goal ②

_____
_____
_____

**What steps do I need to take?**

_____
_____
_____
_____
_____
_____
_____
_____

## Main Goal ③

_____
_____
_____

**What steps do I need to take?**

_____
_____
_____
_____
_____
_____
_____

## Why?

_____
_____

**What is your purpose? What's the 'why' that'll keep you going when times get tough?**

_____
_____
_____
_____
_____
_____

# LEVEL 2

## Uplevel your Daily Habits

It's our daily actions that define our destiny. **The life you are living right now is the accumulation of your daily actions.** If you want to uplevel your life, you don't need one big grand decision - you need to make a lot of really good small decisions - EVERY SINGLE DAY!

Every week you're going to create a new daily routine. You'll follow this routine for the week and then assess/adjust for the next week. Use these habits as

- reminders for things you want to turn into permanent habits
- a way to improve upon existing habits
- a way to try new habits and reflect on their success/failure

It can be the same every week or you can continue to improve and uplevel your actions throughout the year.

Here's some suggestions for activities to use in each area:

 ## Heart

- Meditation
- I am Statements
- Gratitude
- Breathing exercises
- Journaling
- Music - high for energy or soothing for calming... whatever you need!
- Earthing - bare feet in grass
- Motivational Audio Clips
- Silent moments with no distractions

 ## Head

- Self development books
- Self development audio books
- Professional education
- Podcasts

 ## Health

- Exercise - daily walks, morning yoga, gym sessions planned
- Water - are you drinking enough?
- Nutrition - create and follow a food plan
- Sunshine (vitamin D) - go outside
- Sleep routines
- Breath

 ## Relationships

- Scheduled dates
- Daily check-in with loved ones
- Activities towards improving intimacy
- Self care - your relationship with yourself

 ## Mission

Make sure you're taking steps towards your life mission everyday

- Looking at your vision board
- Reading or re-writing your goals
- Planning, creating, researching new projects
- Charity / contribution projects

Make note of the habits you will start implementing into your day...

## Heart

_____
_____
_____
_____
_____
_____
_____
_____
_____
_____
_____

## Health

_____
_____
_____
_____

## Relationships

_____
_____
_____
_____
_____

## Head

_____
_____
_____
_____
_____

## Mission

_____
_____
_____
_____
_____

# LEVEL 3
## It all starts with gratitude

I believe that the fastest pathway to success and happiness, starts with gratitude. We often gauge our level of gratitude on what we have, and feel that we can't be fully grateful until we have what we want. However, the reality is quite the reverse – if we can't be grateful for what we have now, how will we ever be grateful for what we may accomplish.

**Gratitude improves the quality of our life.** There are so many benefits for your mental and physical health. It's been proven time and time again to improve general positivity, improve sleep, increase compassion and kindness towards others and even strengthen immune systems.

**Gratitude can change your life.** It changes our focus on what we have, instead of what we don't have. It can make us appreciate what we do have, even though we're actively working towards having/doing/being more.

**Gratitude can change the way we perceive our daily lives.** When faced with challenging situations, we all react differently. With a perspective of gratitude, we can remain calm in the face of chaos. Things don't always go according to plan, but with an attitude of gratitude, you know that whatever the situation is, we can face it and find some gratitude for the experience. A mindset of gratitude can give you piece of mind.

**Gratitude can set you up for success!** Living in a state of positive energy, sets the scene for you to accept success into your life. Creating a feeling of abundance will attract even more into your life. We attract the feelings and thoughts of things that we are grateful for.

In fact, you can use **gratitude as a manifestation tool**. Feeling grateful for things we don't yet have, can attract some amazing opportunities into your life.

Gratitude won't change your life in one day, but the daily act of being grateful can have an accumulative effect on the way you live your life and what it can attract into your life. Writing it down makes it more real, and actively writing it ensures you participate in gratitude at regular intervals.

You can practice gratitude at any time of the day. Start the day with gratitude and it'll set you up for a better day. End your day with gratitude and you'll have a more peaceful sleep.

Use this journal to express your daily gratitude. You can use the questions on the following page to help begin your journey.

> "Gratitude makes sense of our past, brings peace for today, and creates a vision for tomorrow." – Melody Beattie

*"Gratitude will shift you to a higher frequency,*
***and you will attract much better things."***
– Rhonda Byrne

Think of 3 things you would miss if they were no longer in your life.

_____

_____

_____

What are the 3 smallest things in your daily routine that you could feel happy about, if you truly wanted to?

_____

_____

_____

Think of 3 negative situations that taught you something useful, made you who you are or simply provided a dose of good luck later down the track.

_____

_____

_____

Think of 3 things you complain about that mean you have something wonderful others might not?

_____

_____

_____

Think of a problem you currently have. Write down 1 thing that's good about it, 1 thing you could learn from it and 1 way you can benefit from it.

_____

_____

_____

_____

_____

_____

_____

_____

_____

Write down 3 people who do something to make your life a little easier or enjoyable

_____

_____

_____

## LEVEL 4

# I am Statements

In an earlier section, you decided which attributes and characteristics you would need to help create the life of your dreams.

Now, we begin the process of believing you are the person who lives this life and that you deserve everything you're dreaming and planning.

### Why are 'I am' statements so important?

What follows the two words 'I am' dictates what you believe about yourself, how you show up in the world, and what results you create. Your future success depends on what you believe about yourself. 'I am' statements are really just a list of things you want to do, the person you want to be and feelings you want to have.

### Our thoughts create our reality, our words create our world.

This is so important to understand... YOUR thoughts create YOUR reality, and YOUR words create YOUR world.

What are the statements you currently repeat to yourself when looking in the mirror?

Are you thinking negative thoughts?

Are your thoughts currently supporting the person you want to be, or are they reinforcing the person that you don't want to be?

Are your thoughts supporting your goals or holding you back?

Are you saying you want a certain lifestyle, whilst thinking that you don't deserve it?

### When you say what you want with the words I am in front of them, your subconscious will start to believe what you tell it.

It doesn't know that those things aren't true. If you keep saying and writing them (everyday), you will start to believe them and the universe will work towards creating them.

I want you to have a think about your dreams, look through the heart, head, health, relationships and mission and decide who you need to become to achieve these goals. What person are you right now that doesn't reflect the person you want to be. What behaviours and thought patterns do you need to change to be that person? What words can you start saying to yourself to bridge the gap.

---

Once in a while someone amazing comes along...
*and here I am.*

# Powerful Words to start creating your own 'I am' Statements

| | | | |
|---|---|---|---|
| I am abundant | I am famous | I am kind | I am ready |
| I am active | I am fearless | I am knowledgeable | I am relaxed |
| I am adorable | I am feminine | I am lazer focused | I am resilient |
| I am adored | I am financially savy | I am a leader | I am respected |
| I am affluent | I am fit | I am learning | I am safe |
| I am assertive | I am in the flow | I am legendary | I am sensational |
| I am attractive | I am fortunate | I am light | I am sexy |
| I am authentic | I am free | I am lively | I am shining |
| I am a badass | I am fulfilled | I am love | I am sincere |
| I am beautiful | I am full of energy | I am loved | I am smart |
| I am bighearted | I am generous | I am loving | I am soulful |
| I am blessed | I am genuine | I am loyal | I am spirited |
| I am brilliant | I am gorgeous | I am magical | I am a speaker |
| I am bold | I am graceful | I am masterful | I am special |
| I am brave | I am grateful | I am me | I am splendid |
| I am bright | I am happy | I am a millionaire | I am spontaneous |
| I am calm | I am healed | I am a money magnet | I am strong |
| I am certain | I am healthy | I am natural | I am successful |
| I am charming | I am helpful | I am one of a kind | I am a teacher |
| I am clear | I am honest | I am open | I am thankful |
| I am complete | I am hope | I am optimistic | I am thorough |
| I am confident | I am hilarious | I am organized | I am tranquil |
| I am connected | I am imaginative | I am peaceful | I am trusting |
| I am courageous | I am incredible | I am poised | I am upbeat |
| I am creative | I am independent | I am positive | I am valuable |
| I am curious | I am innovative | I am powerful | I am vibrant |
| I am daring | I am inspired | I am pretty | I am willing |
| I am dedicated | I am an inspiration | I am productive | I am wise |
| I am driven | I am intelligent | I am prosperous | I am whole |
| I am eager | I am intuitive | I am proud | I am wealthy |
| I am effervescent | I am inventive | I am quick | I am wonderful |
| I am enough | I am joy | | I am worthy |
| I am enthusiastic | I am kick ass | | I am youthful |

## LEVEL 5
## Manifest the future

This journal is designed for you to work on becoming the person you need to be to fulfil your wildest dreams. Whilst actively working TOWARDS your dreams, you are also manifesting with your thoughts. You can manifest your dreams by creating a vision for your life and deliberately choosing beliefs, feelings and actions that support that vision.

Here's some ways you can manifest your dream manifesto...

### Gratitude everyday

We're actively doing this daily in this journal. You can add other gratitude activities/exercises to your daily habits.

### Affirmations

Use affirmations with feeling! Write your list of empowering beliefs and fill them in your journal daily. Always write them in the present tense - 'I am.'

### Write your dream

Write about your life in the present tense as if it is happening right now. Describe in great detail all the amazing things that you have and how happy and grateful they make you feel.

Complete this task at the beginning of each month in the journal page provided.

### Create a new identity

Spend time actively thinking about the person you will be when your dreams are realised. How will you act. How will you feel. How will you dress. Create a clear vision in your mind of this version of yourself until it becomes your natural state of being.

### Visualisation

Spend five minutes a day visualising your dream life in as much detail as possible. Where are you? What are you doing? What can you smell. Focus on sensations and feelings.

You will find a page at the beginning of each month to draw your vision.

### De-Clutter

When you hold on to the old, you are not making room for the new in your life. Let go of that which no longer serves you.

### Allow space

Create space in your home, your time, or your office to allow for your dreams to become a reality. Empty a cupboard for your future partner, create files for your future clients. Let the universe know you're ready to accept more.

### Celebrate your wins

Don't be so focused on what's coming up that you don't enjoy the small wins along the way.

# VISION BOARDS & Visualisation

## Layout Ideas!

There's no RULES here! Go with your gut!
✸ Create segments on one sheet as below OR
✸ Create individual boards or pages in a book

## Home
✸ Cleaning / De-cluttering
☆ Home decorating
✸ New Home
✿ Holiday Home
✸ New purchases
✸ Car

## Holidays
✸ Long term
✸ Short term
✸ Local
✿ Overseas
✿ Adventure
✸ Relaxation

## Relationships
✸ Family
✸ Romantic Partner
✿ Children
✿ Extended Family

**Add** Words/Quotes that INSPIRE you or make you FEEL SOMETHING - joy, love, clarity, peace!

*make it rain*

Add a photo of yourself so you can connect with it!

## Health
✸ Lifestyle
✸ Lose weight
✿ Food ideas
✸ Quit smoking
✸ Run 5K
✸ Connecting with self

## Skills/
✸ Education
✸ University
✸ Upskill current skills
✸ Courses
✸ Hobbies
✸ Self Developement
✸ Certificates
✸ Creativity

## Finances
✿ Career
✿ Dream job
✸ Own Business
✸ Work/Life balance
✸ Money Goals
(Don't be scared to put a dollar value to your dreams!!)
✸ Fame/Aspirations
✿ Contribution

Month _____

## Your best year starts now...

### Monthly Goal 1

_____
_____
_____
_____
_____
_____
_____
_____
_____
_____

### Monthly Goal 2

_____
_____
_____
_____
_____
_____
_____
_____
_____
_____

### Monthly Goal 3

_____
_____
_____
_____
_____
_____
_____
_____
_____
_____

### How I will celebrate

_____
_____
_____
_____
_____
_____
_____
_____
_____
_____

# VISION BOARD
Create your vision for the month

**Be** — who do you want to be?

**Do** — what do you want to do?

**Have** — what do you want to have?

**By the end of this month I will...** *(write in the present tense)*

_____
_____
_____
_____
_____
_____
_____
_____
_____
_____

# New week. *New goals.*

Week Start Date [ ]

This week's daily habits

- 🧘 *Heart* _____
- 🧠 *Head* _____
- 🏋 *Health* _____
- 👪 *Relationships* _____
- 🚀 *Mission* _____

*It always seems impossible until it is done.*

Goals for this week
_____
_____
_____

What is my 'WHY'
_____
_____
_____

## Monday

I am
_____
_____
_____
_____
_____
_____

Today's tasks towards my goal
_____
_____
_____

Today I am GRATEFUL for
_____
_____
_____
_____
_____
_____
_____
_____
_____

Daily Habits Checklist  🧘 🧠 🏋 👪 🚀

*I am enough*

# Tuesday

I am
_____
_____
_____
_____
_____

Today's tasks towards my goal
_____
_____
_____

Daily Habits Checklist  ⊛ ⊛ ⊛ ⊛ ⊛

Today I am GRATEFUL for
_____
_____
_____
_____
_____
_____
_____
_____
_____

*I am authentic*

---

# Wednesday

I am
_____
_____
_____
_____
_____

Today's tasks towards my goal
_____
_____
_____

Daily Habits Checklist  ⊛ ⊛ ⊛ ⊛ ⊛

Today I am GRATEFUL for
_____
_____
_____
_____
_____
_____
_____
_____
_____

*I am beautiful*

## Thursday

I am _____

_____
_____
_____
_____
_____

Today's tasks towards my goal

_____
_____
_____

Daily Habits Checklist  ⊙ ⊙ ⊙ ⊙ ⊙

Today I am GRATEFUL for _____

_____
_____
_____
_____
_____
_____
_____
_____
_____

*I am bold*

---

## Friday

I am _____

_____
_____
_____
_____
_____

Today's tasks towards my goal

_____
_____
_____

Daily Habits Checklist  ⊙ ⊙ ⊙ ⊙ ⊙

Today I am GRATEFUL for _____

_____
_____
_____
_____
_____
_____
_____
_____
_____

*I am graceful*

# Saturday

I am _____

_____

_____

_____

_____

_____

Today's tasks towards my goal

_____

_____

_____

Daily Habits Checklist

Today I am GRATEFUL for

_____

_____

_____

_____

_____

_____

_____

*I am successful*

---

# Sunday Reflection

I am GRATEFUL for

_____

_____

What was successful about this week?

_____

_____

What will I do differently?

_____

_____

Thoughts about my daily activities

_____

_____

_____

_____

_____

*I am grateful*

# New week. *New goals.*

Week Start Date ☐

This week's daily habits

- *Heart* _____
- *Head* _____
- *Health* _____
- *Relationships* _____
- *Mission* _____

Goals for this week
_____
_____
_____

What is my 'WHY'
_____
_____

## Monday

I am _____
_____
_____
_____
_____
_____
_____

Today's tasks towards my goal
_____
_____
_____

Today I am GRATEFUL for
_____
_____
_____
_____
_____
_____
_____
_____
_____

Daily Habits Checklist ⊙ ⊙ ⊙ ⊙ ⊙

*I am bright*

# Tuesday

I am _____

_____
_____
_____
_____
_____

Today's tasks towards my goal

_____
_____
_____

Daily Habits Checklist  ⊙ ⊙ ⊙ ⊙ ⊙

Today I am GRATEFUL for _____

_____
_____
_____
_____
_____
_____
_____
_____

*I am bighearted*

---

# Wednesday

I am _____

_____
_____
_____
_____
_____

Today's tasks towards my goal

_____
_____
_____

Daily Habits Checklist  ⊙ ⊙ ⊙ ⊙ ⊙

Today I am GRATEFUL for _____

_____
_____
_____
_____
_____
_____
_____
_____

*I am connected*

## Thursday

I am _____

_____

_____

_____

_____

_____

Today's tasks towards my goal

_____

_____

_____

Daily Habits Checklist ⊙ ⊙ ⊙ ⊙ ⊙

Today I am GRATEFUL for _____

_____

_____

_____

_____

_____

_____

_____

_____

_____

*I am imaginative*

## Friday

I am _____

_____

_____

_____

_____

_____

Today's tasks towards my goal

_____

_____

_____

Daily Habits Checklist ⊙ ⊙ ⊙ ⊙ ⊙

Today I am GRATEFUL for _____

_____

_____

_____

_____

_____

_____

_____

_____

_____

*I am healthy*

# Saturday

I am
_____
_____
_____
_____
_____
_____
_____

Today's tasks towards my goal
_____
_____
_____
_____

Daily Habits Checklist  ⓐ ⓑ ⓒ ⓓ ⓔ

Today I am GRATEFUL for
_____
_____
_____
_____
_____
_____
_____
_____

*I am brilliant*

---

# Sunday Reflection

I am GRATEFUL for
_____
_____

What was successful about this week?
_____
_____

What will I do differently?
_____
_____

Thoughts about my daily activities

ⓐ _____

ⓑ _____

ⓒ _____

ⓓ _____

ⓔ _____

*I am hilarious*

# New week. *New goals.*

Week Start Date _____

This week's daily habits

- *Heart* _____
- *Head* _____
- *Health* _____
- *Relationships* _____
- *Mission* _____

Goals for this week
_____
_____
_____

What is my 'WHY'
_____
_____
_____

## Monday

I am _____
_____
_____
_____
_____
_____

Today's tasks towards my goal
_____
_____

Today I am GRATEFUL for
_____
_____
_____
_____
_____
_____
_____
_____

Daily Habits Checklist

*I am healed*

# Tuesday

I am _____

_____
_____
_____
_____
_____

Today's tasks towards my goal

_____
_____
_____

Daily Habits Checklist  ⊛ ⊛ ⊛ ⊛ ⊛

Today I am GRATEFUL for

_____
_____
_____
_____
_____
_____
_____
_____
_____

*I am confident*

---

# Wednesday

I am _____

_____
_____
_____
_____
_____

Today's tasks towards my goal

_____
_____
_____

Daily Habits Checklist  ⊛ ⊛ ⊛ ⊛ ⊛

Today I am GRATEFUL for

_____
_____
_____
_____
_____
_____

*Happiness doesn't require energy. It requires strategy.*

*I am productive*

## Thursday

I am _____

_____

_____

_____

_____

_____

Today's tasks towards my goal

_____

_____

_____

Daily Habits Checklist  ⚖️ 🧠 ⛺ 👥 🚀

Today I am GRATEFUL for

_____

_____

_____

_____

_____

_____

_____

_____

_____

*I am a Badass*

---

## Friday

I am _____

_____

_____

_____

_____

_____

Today's tasks towards my goal

_____

_____

_____

Daily Habits Checklist  ⚖️ 🧠 ⛺ 👥 🚀

Today I am GRATEFUL for

_____

_____

_____

_____

_____

_____

_____

_____

_____

*I am genuine*

# Saturday

I am
_____
_____
_____
_____
_____
_____

Today's tasks towards my goal
_____
_____
_____

Daily Habits Checklist  ⊛ ⊛ ⊛ ⊛ ⊛

Today I am GRATEFUL for
_____
_____
_____
_____
_____
_____
_____
_____
_____

*I am complete*

---

# Sunday Reflection

I am GRATEFUL for
_____
_____

What was successful about this week?
_____
_____

What will I do differently?
_____
_____

Thoughts about my daily activities

⊛ _____

⊛ _____

⊛ _____

⊛ _____

⊛ _____

*I am honest*

# New week. *New goals.*

Week Start Date [          ]

This week's daily habits

- Heart _____
- Head _____
- Health _____
- Relationships _____
- Mission _____

_____

Goals for this week
_____
_____

What is my 'WHY'
_____
_____

## Monday

I am _____
_____
_____
_____
_____
_____

Today's tasks towards my goal
_____
_____

Daily Habits Checklist

Today I am GRATEFUL for
_____
_____
_____
_____
_____
_____
_____
_____

*I am youthful*

# Tuesday

I am _____

_____
_____
_____
_____
_____

Today's tasks towards my goal

_____
_____
_____

Daily Habits Checklist ○ ○ ○ ○ ○

Today I am GRATEFUL for

_____
_____
_____
_____
_____
_____
_____
_____

*I am independent*

# Wednesday

I am _____

_____
_____
_____
_____
_____

Today's tasks towards my goal

_____
_____
_____

Daily Habits Checklist ○ ○ ○ ○ ○

Today I am GRATEFUL for

_____
_____
_____
_____
_____
_____
_____
_____

*I am inspired*

# Thursday

I am _____

_____
_____
_____
_____
_____

Today's tasks towards my goal

_____
_____
_____

Daily Habits Checklist ⊙ ⊙ ⊙ ⊙ ⊙

Today I am GRATEFUL for

_____
_____
_____
_____
_____
_____
_____
_____
_____

*I am clear*

---

# Friday

I am _____

_____
_____
_____
_____
_____

Today's tasks towards my goal

_____
_____
_____

Daily Habits Checklist ⊙ ⊙ ⊙ ⊙ ⊙

Today I am GRATEFUL for

_____
_____
_____
_____
_____
_____
_____
_____
_____

*I am valuable*

# Saturday

I am _____

_____

_____

_____

_____

_____

Today's tasks towards my goal

_____

_____

_____

Daily Habits Checklist  ⊙ ⊙ ⊙ ⊙ ⊙

Today I am GRATEFUL for

_____

_____

_____

_____

_____

_____

_____

_____

*I am helpful*

---

# Sunday Reflection

I am GRATEFUL for

_____

_____

What was successful about this week?

_____

_____

What will I do differently?

_____

_____

Thoughts about my daily activities

⊙ _____

⊙ _____

⊙ _____

⊙ _____

⊙ _____

*I am peaceful*

Month

# Your best month starts now…

## Monthly Goal 1

## Monthly Goal 2

## Monthly Goal 3

## How I will celebrate

# VISION BOARD
Create your vision for the month

**Be**
who do you want to be?

**Do**
what do you want to do?

**Have**
what do you want to have?

**By the end of this month I will...** *(write in the present tense)*

_____
_____
_____
_____
_____
_____
_____
_____
_____
_____
_____
_____

# New week. *New goals.*

Week Start Date ☐

This week's daily habits

- Heart _____
- Head _____
- Health _____
- Relationships _____
- Mission _____

Goals for this week
_____
_____
_____

What is my 'WHY'
_____
_____
_____

## Monday

I am _____
_____
_____
_____
_____
_____
_____

Today's tasks towards my goal
_____
_____
_____

Daily Habits Checklist ⊙ ⊙ ⊙ ⊙ ⊙

Today I am GRATEFUL for
_____
_____
_____
_____
_____
_____
_____
_____

*I am an inspiration*

# Tuesday

I am _____

_____

_____

_____

_____

_____

_____

Today's tasks towards my goal

_____

_____

Daily Habits Checklist  ⊛ ⊛ ⊛ ⊛ ⊛

Today I am GRATEFUL for

_____

_____

_____

_____

_____

_____

_____

_____

*I am attractive*

---

# Wednesday

I am _____

_____

_____

_____

_____

_____

_____

*You are amazing, you are brave, you are strong.*

Today's tasks towards my goal

_____

_____

Daily Habits Checklist  ⊛ ⊛ ⊛ ⊛ ⊛

Today I am GRATEFUL for

_____

_____

_____

_____

_____

_____

_____

_____

*I am innovative*

# Thursday

I am _____
_____
_____
_____
_____

Today's tasks towards my goal
_____
_____
_____

Daily Habits Checklist  ⊛ ⊛ ⊛ ⊛ ⊛

Today I am GRATEFUL for
_____
_____
_____
_____
_____
_____
_____

*I am charming*

---

# Friday

I am _____
_____
_____
_____
_____

Today's tasks towards my goal
_____
_____
_____

Daily Habits Checklist  ⊛ ⊛ ⊛ ⊛ ⊛

Today I am GRATEFUL for
_____
_____
_____
_____
_____
_____
_____

*I am happy*

# Saturday

I am _____

_____
_____
_____
_____
_____
_____

Today's tasks towards my goal

_____
_____
_____

Daily Habits Checklist  ⬚ ⬚ ⬚ ⬚ ⬚

Today I am GRATEFUL for

_____
_____
_____
_____
_____
_____
_____
_____
_____

*I am certain*

---

# Sunday Reflection

I am GRATEFUL for

_____
_____
_____

What was successful about this week?

_____
_____

What will I do differently?

_____
_____
_____

Thoughts about my daily activities

⬚ _____
_____

⬚ _____
_____

⬚ _____
_____

⬚ _____
_____

⬚ _____
_____

*I am optimistic*

# New week. *New goals.*

Week Start Date _____

This week's daily habits

- Heart _____
- Head _____
- Health _____
- Relationships _____
- Mission _____

Goals for this week
_____
_____
_____

What is my 'WHY'
_____
_____
_____

## Monday

I am _____
_____
_____
_____
_____
_____
_____

Today's tasks towards my goal
_____
_____
_____

Today I am GRATEFUL for
_____
_____
_____
_____
_____
_____
_____
_____
_____

Daily Habits Checklist

*I am blessed*

# Tuesday

I am _____

_____
_____
_____
_____
_____
_____

Today's tasks towards my goal

_____
_____
_____

Daily Habits Checklist  ⊛ ⊛ ⊛ ⊛ ⊛

Today I am GRATEFUL for

_____
_____
_____
_____
_____
_____
_____
_____
_____

*I am lazer focused*

---

# Wednesday

I am _____

_____
_____
_____
_____
_____
_____

Today's tasks towards my goal

_____
_____
_____

Daily Habits Checklist  ⊛ ⊛ ⊛ ⊛ ⊛

Today I am GRATEFUL for

_____
_____
_____
_____
_____
_____
_____
_____
_____

*I am courageous*

## Thursday

I am _____

_____

_____

_____

_____

_____

Today's tasks towards my goal

_____

_____

_____

Daily Habits Checklist  ⓐ ⓑ ⓒ ⓓ ⓔ

Today I am GRATEFUL for
_____

_____

_____

_____

_____

_____

_____

_____

_____

*I am enthusiastic*

---

## Friday

I am _____

_____

_____

_____

_____

_____

Today's tasks towards my goal

_____

_____

_____

Daily Habits Checklist  ⓐ ⓑ ⓒ ⓓ ⓔ

Today I am GRATEFUL for
_____

_____

_____

_____

_____

_____

_____

_____

_____

*I am brave*

# Saturday

I am _____

_____

_____

_____

_____

_____

Today's tasks towards my goal

_____

_____

_____

Daily Habits Checklist

Today I am GRATEFUL for

_____

_____

_____

_____

_____

_____

_____

_____

*I am trusting*

---

# Sunday Reflection

I am GRATEFUL for

_____

_____

What was successful about this week?

_____

_____

What will I do differently?

_____

_____

_____

Thoughts about my daily activities

_____

_____

_____

_____

_____

*I am a speaker*

# New week. *New goals.*

Week Start Date [ ]

This week's daily habits

- *Heart* _____
- *Head* _____
- *Health* _____
- *Relationships* _____
- *Mission* _____

Goals for this week
_____
_____
_____

What is my 'WHY'
_____
_____
_____

## Monday

I am
_____
_____
_____
_____
_____
_____
_____

Today's tasks towards my goal
_____
_____
_____

Daily Habits Checklist

Today I am GRATEFUL for
_____
_____
_____
_____
_____
_____
_____
_____

*I am famous*

## Tuesday

I am _____
_____
_____
_____
_____
_____

Today's tasks towards my goal
_____
_____
_____

Daily Habits Checklist  ⊕ ⊕ ⊕ ⊕ ⊕

| Today I am GRATEFUL for |
| --- |
| _____ |
| _____ |
| _____ |
| _____ |
| _____ |
| _____ |
| _____ |
| _____ |

*I am masterful*

---

## Wednesday

I am _____
_____
_____
_____
_____
_____

Today's tasks towards my goal
_____
_____
_____

Daily Habits Checklist  ⊕ ⊕ ⊕ ⊕ ⊕

| Today I am GRATEFUL for |
| --- |
| _____ |
| _____ |
| _____ |
| _____ |
| _____ |
| _____ |
| _____ |
| _____ |

*I am magical*

## Thursday

I am _____

_____

_____

_____

_____

_____

Today's tasks towards my goal

_____

_____

_____

Daily Habits Checklist  ⊘ ⊘ ⊘ ⊘ ⊘

Today I am GRATEFUL for

_____

_____

_____

_____

_____

_____

_____

_____

*I am calm*

---

## Friday

I am _____

_____

_____

_____

_____

*You are gold, baby. Solid gold.*

Today's tasks towards my goal

_____

_____

_____

Daily Habits Checklist  ⊘ ⊘ ⊘ ⊘ ⊘

Today I am GRATEFUL for

_____

_____

_____

_____

_____

_____

_____

_____

*I am assertive*

# Saturday

I am _____

_____
_____
_____
_____
_____

Today's tasks towards my goal

_____
_____
_____

Daily Habits Checklist  ⊙ ⊙ ⊙ ⊙ ⊙

Today I am GRATEFUL for

_____
_____
_____
_____
_____
_____
_____
_____
_____

*I am daring*

---

# Sunday Reflection

I am GRATEFUL for

_____
_____

What was successful about this week?

_____
_____

What will I do differently?

_____
_____
_____

Thoughts about my daily activities

⊙ _____

⊙ _____

⊙ _____

⊙ _____

⊙ _____

*I am enough*

# New week. *New goals.*

Week Start Date ☐

This week's daily habits

- *Heart* _____
- *Head* _____
- *Health* _____
- *Relationships* _____
- *Mission* _____

Goals for this week
_____
_____
_____

What is my 'WHY'
_____
_____
_____

# Monday

I am _____
_____
_____
_____
_____
_____
_____

Today's tasks towards my goal
_____
_____
_____

Daily Habits Checklist  ⓢ ⓟ ⓗ ⓡ ⓜ

Today I am GRATEFUL for
_____
_____
_____
_____
_____
_____
_____
_____
_____

*I am loyal*

# Tuesday

I am _____

_____

_____

_____

_____

_____

Today's tasks towards my goal

_____

_____

_____

Daily Habits Checklist  ⓐ ⓑ ⓒ ⓓ ⓔ

Today I am GRATEFUL for _____

_____

_____

_____

_____

_____

_____

_____

_____

*I am a millionaire*

---

# Wednesday

I am _____

_____

_____

_____

_____

_____

Today's tasks towards my goal

_____

_____

_____

Daily Habits Checklist  ⓐ ⓑ ⓒ ⓓ ⓔ

Today I am GRATEFUL for _____

_____

_____

_____

_____

_____

_____

_____

_____

*I am loving*

# Thursday

I am _____

_____

_____

_____

_____

_____

Today's tasks towards my goal

_____

_____

_____

Daily Habits Checklist  🍽 🧠 🧘 🎨 🚀

Today I am GRATEFUL for

_____

_____

_____

_____

_____

_____

_____

_____

_____

*I am tranquil*

---

# Friday

I am _____

_____

_____

_____

_____

_____

Today's tasks towards my goal

_____

_____

_____

Daily Habits Checklist  🍽 🧠 🧘 🎨 🚀

Today I am GRATEFUL for

_____

_____

_____

_____

_____

_____

_____

_____

_____

*I am creative*

# Saturday

I am _____

_____

_____

_____

_____

_____

Today's tasks towards my goal

_____

_____

_____

Daily Habits Checklist

Today I am GRATEFUL for _____

_____

_____

_____

_____

_____

_____

_____

_____

*I am legendary*

---

# Sunday Reflection

I am GRATEFUL for

_____

_____

_____

What was successful about this week?

_____

_____

What will I do differently?

_____

_____

_____

Thoughts about my daily activities

_____

_____

_____

_____

_____

*I am lively*

Month

# Keep going...

## Monthly Goal 1

_____
_____
_____
_____
_____
_____
_____
_____
_____

## Monthly Goal 2

_____
_____
_____
_____
_____
_____
_____
_____
_____

## Monthly Goal 3

_____
_____
_____
_____
_____
_____
_____
_____

## How I will celebrate

_____
_____
_____
_____
_____
_____
_____
_____

# VISION BOARD
Create your vision for the month

### Be
who do you want to be?

### Do
what do you want to do?

### Have
what do you want to have?

**By the end of this month I will...** *(write in the present tense)*

_____
_____
_____
_____
_____
_____
_____
_____
_____

# New week. *New goals.*

Week Start Date _____

This week's daily habits

- *Heart* _____
- *Head* _____
- *Health* _____
- *Relationships* _____
- *Mission* _____

Goals for this week                                          *Don't think, just do - Horace*
_____
_____
_____

What is my 'WHY'
_____
_____
_____

# Monday

I am _____
_____
_____
_____
_____
_____
_____

Today's tasks towards my goal
_____
_____
_____

Daily Habits Checklist

Today I am GRATEFUL for
_____
_____
_____
_____
_____
_____
_____
_____
_____

*I am curious*

# Tuesday

I am _____
_____
_____
_____
_____
_____

Today's tasks towards my goal
_____
_____
_____

Daily Habits Checklist  ⊙ ⊙ ⊙ ⊙ ⊙

Today I am GRATEFUL for
_____
_____
_____
_____
_____
_____
_____

*I am effervescent*

---

# Wednesday

I am _____
_____
_____
_____
_____
_____

Today's tasks towards my goal
_____
_____
_____

Daily Habits Checklist  ⊙ ⊙ ⊙ ⊙ ⊙

Today I am GRATEFUL for
_____
_____
_____
_____
_____
_____
_____

*I am thorough*

# Thursday

I am _____

_____
_____
_____
_____
_____

Today's tasks towards my goal

_____
_____
_____

Daily Habits Checklist  ⊘ ⊘ ⊘ ⊘ ⊘

Today I am GRATEFUL for

_____
_____
_____
_____
_____
_____
_____
_____

*I am dedicate*

---

# Friday

I am _____

_____
_____
_____
_____
_____

Today's tasks towards my goal

_____
_____
_____

Daily Habits Checklist  ⊘ ⊘ ⊘ ⊘ ⊘

Today I am GRATEFUL for

_____
_____
_____
_____
_____
_____
_____
_____

*I am full of energy*

# Saturday

I am _____

_____
_____
_____
_____
_____

Today I am GRATEFUL for _____

_____
_____
_____
_____
_____

Today's tasks towards my goal

_____
_____
_____

_____
_____
_____

Daily Habits Checklist ⚪ ⚪ ⚪ ⚪ ⚪

*I am generous*

---

# Sunday Reflection

I am GRATEFUL for

_____
_____

What was successful about this week?

_____
_____

What will I do differently?

_____
_____
_____

Thoughts about my daily activities

⚪ _____

⚪ _____

⚪ _____

⚪ _____

⚪ _____

*I am gorgeous*

# New week. *New goals.*

Week Start Date _____

This week's daily habits

- *Heart* _____
- *Head* _____
- *Health* _____
- *Relationships* _____
- *Mission* _____

*Be a pineapple stand tall wear a crown and be sweet on the inside.*

Goals for this week
_____
_____
_____

What is my 'WHY'
_____
_____
_____

## Monday

I am
_____
_____
_____
_____
_____
_____

Today's tasks towards my goal
_____
_____
_____

Today I am GRATEFUL for
_____
_____
_____
_____
_____
_____
_____
_____

Daily Habits Checklist

*I am quirky*

# Tuesday

I am _____

_____

_____

_____

_____

_____

_____

Today's tasks towards my goal

_____

_____

Daily Habits Checklist

Today I am GRATEFUL for

_____

_____

_____

_____

_____

_____

_____

_____

_____

*I am fearless*

---

# Wednesday

I am _____

_____

_____

_____

_____

_____

_____

Today's tasks towards my goal

_____

_____

Daily Habits Checklist

Today I am GRATEFUL for

_____

_____

_____

_____

_____

_____

_____

_____

_____

*I am wonderful*

# Thursday

I am _____

_____

_____

_____

_____

_____

Today's tasks towards my goal

_____

_____

_____

Daily Habits Checklist  ⚪ ⚪ ⚪ ⚪ ⚪

Today I am GRATEFUL for

_____

_____

_____

_____

_____

_____

_____

_____

*I am worthy*

---

# Friday

I am _____

_____

_____

_____

_____

_____

Today's tasks towards my goal

_____

_____

_____

Daily Habits Checklist  ⚪ ⚪ ⚪ ⚪ ⚪

Today I am GRATEFUL for

_____

_____

_____

_____

_____

_____

_____

_____

*I am wise*

# Saturday

I am _____

_____

_____

_____

_____

_____

Today's tasks towards my goal

_____

_____

_____

Daily Habits Checklist  ⚬ ⚬ ⚬ ⚬ ⚬

Today I am GRATEFUL for _____

_____

_____

_____

_____

_____

_____

_____

*I am hope*

---

# Sunday Reflection

I am GRATEFUL for

_____

_____

What was successful about this week?

_____

_____

What will I do differently?

_____

_____

Thoughts about my daily activities

⚬ _____

⚬ _____

⚬ _____

⚬ _____

⚬ _____

*I am financially savy*

# New week. *New goals.*

**Week Start Date** ☐

This week's daily habits

- *Heart* _____
- *Head* _____
- *Health* _____
- *Relationships* _____
- *Mission* _____

Goals for this week
_____
_____
_____

What is my 'WHY'
_____
_____
_____

## Monday

I am
_____
_____
_____
_____
_____
_____

Today's tasks towards my goal
_____
_____
_____

Daily Habits Checklist

Today I am GRATEFUL for
_____
_____
_____
_____
_____
_____
_____
_____

*I am fit*

# Tuesday

I am _____

_____

_____

_____

_____

_____

Today's tasks towards my goal

_____

_____

Daily Habits Checklist  ⊘ ⊘ ⊘ ⊘ ⊘

Today I am GRATEFUL for _____

_____

_____

_____

_____

_____

_____

_____

*I am incredible*

---

# Wednesday

I am _____

_____

_____

_____

_____

*You are capable of amazing things.*

Today's tasks towards my goal

_____

_____

Daily Habits Checklist  ⊘ ⊘ ⊘ ⊘ ⊘

Today I am GRATEFUL for _____

_____

_____

_____

_____

_____

_____

_____

*I am feminine*

# Thursday

I am _____
_____
_____
_____
_____
_____

Today's tasks towards my goal
_____
_____
_____

Daily Habits Checklist  ⓘ ⓘ ⓘ ⓘ ⓘ

Today I am GRATEFUL for
_____
_____
_____
_____
_____
_____
_____

*I am inventive*

# Friday

I am _____
_____
_____
_____
_____
_____

Today's tasks towards my goal
_____
_____
_____

Daily Habits Checklist  ⓘ ⓘ ⓘ ⓘ ⓘ

Today I am GRATEFUL for
_____
_____
_____
_____
_____
_____
_____

*I am prosperous*

# Saturday

I am _____

_____
_____
_____
_____
_____
_____

Today's tasks towards my goal

_____
_____
_____

Daily Habits Checklist  ⊙ ⊙ ⊙ ⊙ ⊙

Today I am GRATEFUL for

_____
_____
_____
_____
_____
_____
_____
_____
_____
_____

*I am intelligent*

# Sunday Reflection

I am GRATEFUL for

_____
_____

What was successful about this week?

_____
_____

What will I do differently?

_____
_____

Thoughts about my daily activities

⊙ _____
⊙ _____
⊙ _____
⊙ _____
⊙ _____

*I am fortunate*

# New week. *New goals.*

**Week Start Date**

This week's daily habits

- *Heart* _____
- *Head* _____
- *Health* _____
- *Relationships* _____
- *Mission* _____

Goals for this week
_____
_____
_____

What is my 'WHY'
_____
_____
_____

## Monday

I am
_____
_____
_____
_____
_____
_____

Today's tasks towards my goal
_____
_____
_____

Today I am GRATEFUL for
_____
_____
_____
_____
_____
_____
_____
_____

Daily Habits Checklist

*I am learning*

# Tuesday

I am _____

_____
_____
_____
_____
_____

Today's tasks towards my goal

_____
_____

Daily Habits Checklist  ◯ ◯ ◯ ◯ ◯

Today I am GRATEFUL for
_____
_____
_____
_____
_____
_____
_____
_____
_____

*I am fulfilled*

---

# Wednesday

I am _____

_____
_____
_____
_____
_____

Today's tasks towards my goal

_____
_____

Daily Habits Checklist  ◯ ◯ ◯ ◯ ◯

Today I am GRATEFUL for
_____
_____
_____
_____
_____
_____
_____
_____
_____

*I am shining*

# Thursday

I am _____

_____

_____

_____

_____

Today's tasks towards my goal

_____

_____

Daily Habits Checklist  ⊕ ⊕ ⊕ ⊕ ⊕

Today I am GRATEFUL for
_____

_____

_____

_____

_____

_____

_____

*I am in the flow*

---

# Friday

I am _____

_____

_____

_____

_____

Today's tasks towards my goal

_____

_____

Daily Habits Checklist  ⊕ ⊕ ⊕ ⊕ ⊕

Today I am GRATEFUL for
_____

_____

_____

_____

_____

_____

_____

*I am free*

# Saturday

I am _____

_____

_____

_____

_____

_____

Today's tasks towards my goal

_____

_____

Daily Habits Checklist

Today I am GRATEFUL for _____

_____

_____

_____

_____

_____

_____

_____

*I am a leader*

---

# Sunday Reflection

I am GRATEFUL for

_____

_____

What was successful about this week?

_____

_____

What will I do differently?

_____

_____

Thoughts about my daily activities

_____

_____

_____

_____

_____

*I am knowledgeable*

# New week. *New goals.*

Week Start Date [ ]

This week's daily habits

- *Heart* _____
- *Head* _____
- *Health* _____
- *Relationships* _____
- *Mission* _____

Goals for this week
_____
_____
_____

What is my 'WHY'
_____
_____
_____

## Monday

I am _____
_____
_____
_____
_____
_____

Today's tasks towards my goal
_____
_____
_____

Daily Habits Checklist

Today I am GRATEFUL for
_____
_____
_____
_____
_____
_____
_____
_____

*I am eager*

# Tuesday

I am _____

_____

_____

_____

_____

_____

_____

Today's tasks towards my goal

_____

_____

Daily Habits Checklist  ⊛ ⊛ ⊛ ⊛ ⊛

Today I am GRATEFUL for

_____

_____

_____

_____

_____

_____

_____

_____

_____

*I am sensational*

---

# Wednesday

I am _____

_____

_____

_____

_____

_____

_____

Today's tasks towards my goal

_____

_____

Daily Habits Checklist  ⊛ ⊛ ⊛ ⊛ ⊛

Today I am GRATEFUL for

_____

_____

_____

_____

_____

_____

_____

_____

_____

*I am kind*

## Thursday

I am _____

_____

_____

_____

_____

Today's tasks towards my goal

_____

_____

Daily Habits Checklist  ⊛ ⊛ ⊛ ⊛ ⊛

Today I am GRATEFUL for

_____

_____

_____

_____

_____

_____

_____

*I am quick*

---

## Friday

I am _____

_____

_____

_____

_____

Today's tasks towards my goal

_____

_____

Daily Habits Checklist  ⊛ ⊛ ⊛ ⊛ ⊛

Today I am GRATEFUL for

_____

_____

_____

_____

_____

_____

_____

*I am relaxed*

# Saturday

I am _____

_____
_____
_____
_____
_____

Today I am GRATEFUL for

_____
_____
_____
_____
_____
_____

Today's tasks towards my goal

_____
_____
_____

Daily Habits Checklist 🎂 🧠 🧘 👥 🚀

*I am sincere*

---

# Sunday Reflection

I am GRATEFUL for

_____
_____

What was successful about this week?

_____
_____

What will I do differently?

_____
_____

Thoughts about my daily activities

🎂 _____

🧠 _____

🧘 _____

👥 _____

🚀 _____

*You only fail when you stop trying.*

*I am intuitive*

Month _____

# Keep going...

## Monthly Goal ①

_____
_____
_____
_____
_____
_____
_____
_____
_____
_____

## Monthly Goal ②

_____
_____
_____
_____
_____
_____
_____
_____
_____
_____

## Monthly Goal ③

_____
_____
_____
_____
_____
_____
_____
_____
_____
_____

## How I will celebrate

_____
_____
_____
_____
_____
_____
_____
_____
_____
_____

# VISION BOARD
Create your vision for the month

**Be** — who do you want to be?

**Do** — what do you want to do?

**Have** — what do you want to have?

**By the end of this month I will...** *(write in the present tense)*

_____
_____
_____
_____
_____
_____
_____
_____
_____
_____
_____

# New week. *New goals.*

Week Start Date ☐

This week's daily habits

- *Heart* _____
- *Head* _____
- *Health* _____
- *Relationships* _____
- *Mission* _____

Goals for this week
_____
_____
_____

What is my 'WHY'
_____
_____

## Monday

I am _____
_____
_____
_____
_____
_____

Today's tasks towards my goal
_____
_____
_____

Daily Habits Checklist

Today I am GRATEFUL for
_____
_____
_____
_____
_____
_____
_____
_____

*I am driven*

# Tuesday

I am _____

_____

_____

_____

_____

_____

Today's tasks towards my goal

_____

_____

_____

Daily Habits Checklist   ⓐ ⓑ ⓒ ⓓ ⓔ

Today I am GRATEFUL for

_____

_____

_____

_____

_____

_____

_____

_____

_____

*I am whole*

---

# Wednesday

I am _____

_____

_____

_____

_____

*I believe in you.*

Today's tasks towards my goal

_____

_____

_____

Daily Habits Checklist   ⓐ ⓑ ⓒ ⓓ ⓔ

Today I am GRATEFUL for

_____

_____

_____

_____

_____

_____

_____

_____

_____

*I am wealthy*

# Thursday

I am _____

_____

_____

_____

_____

_____

Today's tasks towards my goal

_____

_____

_____

Daily Habits Checklist  ⊙ ⊙ ⊙ ⊙ ⊙

Today I am GRATEFUL for

_____

_____

_____

_____

_____

_____

_____

_____

_____

*I am organized*

---

# Friday

I am _____

_____

_____

_____

_____

_____

Today's tasks towards my goal

_____

_____

_____

Daily Habits Checklist  ⊙ ⊙ ⊙ ⊙ ⊙

Today I am GRATEFUL for

_____

_____

_____

_____

_____

_____

_____

_____

_____

*I am love*

# Saturday

I am _____

_____

_____

_____

_____

_____

Today's tasks towards my goal

_____

_____

_____

Daily Habits Checklist  ⊙ ⊙ ⊙ ⊙ ⊙

Today I am GRATEFUL for

_____

_____

_____

_____

_____

_____

_____

_____

*I am poised*

---

# Sunday Reflection

I am GRATEFUL for

_____

_____

What was successful about this week?

_____

_____

What will I do differently?

_____

_____

Thoughts about my daily activities

⊙ _____

⊙ _____

⊙ _____

⊙ _____

⊙ _____

*I am positive*

# New week. *New goals.*

**Week Start Date** ☐

This week's daily habits

- Heart _____
- Head _____
- Health _____
- Relationships _____
- Mission _____

*Expect problems and eat them for breakfast - A Montapert*

**Goals for this week**
_____
_____
_____

**What is my 'WHY'**
_____
_____

## Monday

**I am**
_____
_____
_____
_____
_____
_____

**Today's tasks towards my goal**
_____
_____
_____

**Today I am GRATEFUL for**
_____
_____
_____
_____
_____
_____
_____
_____
_____

**Daily Habits Checklist** ⊙ ⊙ ⊙ ⊙ ⊙   *I am me*

# Tuesday

I am _____

_____

_____

_____

_____

_____

Today's tasks towards my goal

_____

_____

Daily Habits Checklist  ⊛ ⊚ ⊠ ⊛ ⊛

Today I am GRATEFUL for

_____

_____

_____

_____

_____

_____

_____

_____

*I am loved*

---

# Wednesday

I am _____

_____

_____

_____

_____

_____

Today's tasks towards my goal

_____

_____

Daily Habits Checklist  ⊛ ⊚ ⊠ ⊛ ⊛

Today I am GRATEFUL for

_____

_____

_____

_____

_____

_____

_____

_____

*I am natural*

# Thursday

I am _____
_____
_____
_____
_____
_____

Today's tasks towards my goal
_____
_____
_____

Daily Habits Checklist  ⊛ ⊛ ⊛ ⊛ ⊛

Today I am GRATEFUL for
_____
_____
_____
_____
_____
_____
_____
_____
_____

*I am powerful*

---

# Friday

I am _____ *You are way more than enough.*
_____
_____
_____
_____
_____
_____

Today's tasks towards my goal
_____
_____
_____

Daily Habits Checklist  ⊛ ⊛ ⊛ ⊛ ⊛

Today I am GRATEFUL for
_____
_____
_____
_____
_____
_____
_____
_____
_____

*I am open*

# Saturday

I am _____

_____
_____
_____
_____
_____
_____

Today's tasks towards my goal

_____
_____
_____

Daily Habits Checklist  ⊛ ⊚ ⊛ ⊛ ⊛

Today I am GRATEFUL for

_____
_____
_____
_____
_____
_____
_____
_____
_____
_____

*I am pretty*

---

# Sunday Reflection

I am GRATEFUL for

_____
_____

What was successful about this week?

_____
_____

What will I do differently?

_____
_____

Thoughts about my daily activities

⊛ _____
⊚ _____
⊛ _____
⊛ _____
⊛ _____

*I am a money magnet*

# New week. *New goals.*

Week Start Date _____

This week's daily habits

- *Heart* _____
- *Head* _____
- *Health* _____
- *Relationships* _____
- *Mission* _____

_____

Goals for this week
_____
_____
_____

What is my 'WHY'
_____
_____
_____

## Monday

I am _____ | Today I am GRATEFUL for
_____ | _____
_____ | _____
_____ | _____
_____ | _____
_____ | _____
_____ | _____

Today's tasks towards my goal
_____ | _____
_____ | _____
_____ | _____

Daily Habits Checklist  ⊙ ⊙ ⊙ ⊙ ⊙           *I am one of a kind*

# Tuesday

I am _____

_____

_____

_____

_____

_____

Today's tasks towards my goal

_____

_____

_____

Daily Habits Checklist  ⊛ ⊛ ⊛ ⊛ ⊛

Today I am GRATEFUL for _____

_____

_____

_____

_____

_____

_____

_____

_____

_____

*I am light*

---

# Wednesday

I am _____

_____

_____

_____

_____

_____

Today's tasks towards my goal

_____

_____

_____

Daily Habits Checklist  ⊛ ⊛ ⊛ ⊛ ⊛

Today I am GRATEFUL for _____

_____

_____

_____

_____

_____

_____

_____

_____

_____

*I am kick ass*

# Thursday

I am _____

_____

_____

_____

_____

_____

Today's tasks towards my goal

_____

_____

Daily Habits Checklist  ⊛ ⊛ ⊛ ⊛ ⊛

Today I am GRATEFUL for

_____

_____

_____

_____

_____

_____

_____

_____

*I am willing*

---

# Friday

I am _____

_____

_____

_____

_____

_____

Today's tasks towards my goal

_____

_____

Daily Habits Checklist  ⊛ ⊛ ⊛ ⊛ ⊛

Today I am GRATEFUL for

_____

_____

_____

_____

_____

_____

_____

_____

*I am thankful*

# Saturday

I am _____

_____

_____

_____

_____

_____

Today's tasks towards my goal

_____

_____

_____

Daily Habits Checklist  ⊛ ⊛ ⊛ ⊛ ⊛

Today I am GRATEFUL for _____

_____

_____

_____

_____

_____

_____

*Your smile lights up the room.*

*I am resilient*

---

# Sunday Reflection

I am GRATEFUL for

_____

_____

What was successful about this week?

_____

_____

What will I do differently?

_____

_____

Thoughts about my daily activities

⊛ _____

⊛ _____

⊛ _____

⊛ _____

⊛ _____

*I am safe*

# New week. *New goals.*

Week Start Date [          ]

This week's daily habits

- *Heart* _____
- *Head* _____
- *Health* _____
- *Relationships* _____
- *Mission* _____

*In case you forgot to remind yourself this morning: Your butt is perfect.*

Goals for this week
_____
_____
_____

What is my 'WHY'
_____
_____

---

## Monday

I am _____
_____
_____
_____
_____
_____

Today's tasks towards my goal
_____
_____
_____

Daily Habits Checklist  ⓢ ⓗ ⓗ ⓡ ⓜ

Today I am GRATEFUL for
_____
_____
_____
_____
_____
_____
_____
_____

*I am smart*

## Tuesday

I am _____

_____
_____
_____
_____
_____
_____

Today's tasks towards my goal

_____
_____
_____

Daily Habits Checklist  ⓐ ⓑ ⓒ ⓓ ⓔ

Today I am GRATEFUL for
_____
_____
_____
_____
_____
_____
_____
_____

*I am joy*

---

## Wednesday

I am _____

_____
_____
_____
_____
_____
_____

Today's tasks towards my goal

_____
_____
_____

Daily Habits Checklist  ⓐ ⓑ ⓒ ⓓ ⓔ

Today I am GRATEFUL for
_____
_____
_____
_____
_____
_____
_____
_____

*I am respected*

# Thursday

I am _____

_____
_____
_____
_____
_____

Today's tasks towards my goal

_____
_____

Daily Habits Checklist  ⓐ ⓑ ⓒ ⓓ ⓔ

Today I am GRATEFUL for
_____
_____
_____
_____
_____
_____
_____
_____
_____

*I am abundant*

---

# Friday

I am _____

_____
_____
_____
_____
_____

Today's tasks towards my goal

_____
_____

Daily Habits Checklist  ⓐ ⓑ ⓒ ⓓ ⓔ

Today I am GRATEFUL for
_____
_____
_____
_____
_____
_____
_____
_____
_____

*I am ready*

# Saturday

I am _____

_____

_____

_____

_____

_____

Today's tasks towards my goal

_____

_____

_____

Daily Habits Checklist  ⊙ ⊙ ⊙ ⊙ ⊙

Today I am GRATEFUL for

_____

_____

_____

_____

_____

_____

_____

_____

_____

*I am active*

---

# Sunday Reflection

I am GRATEFUL for

_____

_____

What was successful about this week?

_____

_____

What will I do differently?

_____

_____

_____

Thoughts about my daily activities

⊙ _____

⊙ _____

⊙ _____

⊙ _____

⊙ _____

*I am spirited*

Month ▢

## You've got this...

### Monthly Goal ①

_____
_____
_____
_____
_____
_____
_____
_____
_____

### Monthly Goal ②

_____
_____
_____
_____
_____
_____
_____
_____
_____

### Monthly Goal ③

_____
_____
_____
_____
_____
_____
_____
_____
_____

### How I will celebrate

_____
_____
_____
_____
_____
_____
_____
_____
_____

# VISION BOARD
Create your vision for the month

**Be**
who do you want to be?

**Do**
what do you want to do?

**Have**
what do you want to have?

**By the end of this month I will...** *(write in the present tense)*

_____
_____
_____
_____
_____
_____
_____
_____
_____
_____
_____

# New week. *New goals.*

Week Start Date _____

This week's daily habits

- Heart _____
- Head _____
- Health _____
- Relationships _____
- Mission _____

Goals for this week
_____
_____
_____

What is my 'WHY'
_____
_____
_____

## Monday

I am _____
_____
_____
_____
_____
_____

Today's tasks towards my goal
_____
_____

Today I am GRATEFUL for
_____
_____
_____
_____
_____
_____
_____
_____

Daily Habits Checklist

*I am proud*

## Tuesday

I am _____

_____

_____

_____

_____

_____

Today's tasks towards my goal     *Never give up!*

_____

_____

_____

Daily Habits Checklist  ⓐ ⓑ ⓒ ⓓ ⓔ

Today I am GRATEFUL for _____

_____

_____

_____

_____

_____

_____

_____

_____

*I am sexy*

---

## Wednesday

I am _____

_____

_____

_____

_____

_____

Today's tasks towards my goal

_____

_____

_____

Daily Habits Checklist  ⓐ ⓑ ⓒ ⓓ ⓔ

Today I am GRATEFUL for _____

_____

_____

_____

_____

_____

_____

_____

_____

*I am adorable*

# Thursday

I am _____

_____
_____
_____
_____
_____

Today's tasks towards my goal

_____
_____

Daily Habits Checklist  ○ ○ ○ ○ ○

Today I am GRATEFUL for
_____
_____
_____
_____
_____
_____
_____
_____
_____

*I am affluent*

---

# Friday

I am _____

_____
_____
_____
_____
_____

Today's tasks towards my goal

_____
_____

Daily Habits Checklist  ○ ○ ○ ○ ○

Today I am GRATEFUL for
_____
_____
_____
_____
_____
_____
_____
_____
_____

*I am soulful*

# Saturday

I am _____

_____
_____
_____
_____
_____
_____

*Your mind is insanely cool.*

Today's tasks towards my goal

_____
_____
_____
_____

Daily Habits Checklist  ⓐ ⓑ ⓒ ⓓ ⓔ

Today I am GRATEFUL for _____

_____
_____
_____
_____
_____
_____
_____

*I am vibrant*

---

# Sunday Reflection

I am GRATEFUL for

_____
_____

What was successful about this week?

_____
_____

What will I do differently?

_____
_____

Thoughts about my daily activities

ⓐ _____

ⓑ _____

ⓒ _____

ⓓ _____

ⓔ _____

*I am upbeat*

# New week. *New goals.*

Week Start Date _____

This week's daily habits

- *Heart* _____
- *Head* _____
- *Health* _____
- *Relationships* _____
- *Mission* _____

*Whenever you doubt how far you can go, just remember how far you have come.*

**Goals for this week**
_____
_____
_____

**What is my 'WHY'**
_____
_____
_____

## Monday

I am _____
_____
_____
_____
_____
_____

Today's tasks towards my goal
_____
_____
_____

Today I am GRATEFUL for
_____
_____
_____
_____
_____
_____
_____
_____
_____

Daily Habits Checklist

*I am a teacher*

# Tuesday

I am _____

_____

_____

_____

_____

_____

Today's tasks towards my goal

_____

_____

_____

Daily Habits Checklist  ⓐ ⓑ ⓒ ⓓ ⓔ

Today I am GRATEFUL for

_____

_____

_____

_____

_____

_____

_____

_____

*I am spontaneous*

---

# Wednesday

I am _____

_____

_____

_____

_____

_____

Today's tasks towards my goal

_____

_____

_____

Daily Habits Checklist  ⓐ ⓑ ⓒ ⓓ ⓔ

Today I am GRATEFUL for

_____

_____

_____

_____

_____

_____

_____

_____

*I am strong*

## Thursday

I am _____

_____
_____
_____
_____
_____
_____

Today's tasks towards my goal

_____
_____
_____

Daily Habits Checklist  ⊛ ⊛ ⊛ ⊛ ⊛

Today I am GRATEFUL for

_____
_____
_____
_____
_____
_____
_____
_____

*I am special*

---

## Friday

I am _____

_____
_____
_____
_____
_____
_____

Today's tasks towards my goal

_____
_____
_____

Daily Habits Checklist  ⊛ ⊛ ⊛ ⊛ ⊛

Today I am GRATEFUL for

_____
_____
_____
_____
_____
_____
_____
_____

*I am a Badass*

# Saturday

I am _____

_____
_____
_____
_____
_____

Today's tasks towards my goal

_____
_____
_____

Daily Habits Checklist  ⊘ ⊘ ⊘ ⊘ ⊘

Today I am GRATEFUL for

_____
_____
_____
_____
_____
_____
_____
_____

*I am splendid*

---

# Sunday Reflection

I am GRATEFUL for

_____
_____

What was successful about this week?

_____
_____

What will I do differently?

_____
_____

Thoughts about my daily activities

⊘ _____

⊘ _____

⊘ _____

⊘ _____

⊘ _____

*I am Beautiful*

# New week. *New goals.*

**Week Start Date**

This week's daily habits

- *Heart* _____
- *Head* _____
- *Health* _____
- *Relationships* _____
- *Mission* _____

Goals for this week
_____
_____
_____

What is my 'WHY'
_____
_____
_____

## Monday

I am _____
_____
_____
_____
_____
_____

Today's tasks towards my goal
_____
_____
_____

Daily Habits Checklist

Today I am GRATEFUL for
_____
_____
_____
_____
_____
_____
_____
_____
_____

*I am full of energy*

# Tuesday

I am _____

_____
_____
_____
_____
_____

Today I am GRATEFUL for

_____
_____
_____
_____
_____
_____

*You are doing an amazing job at life.*

Today's tasks towards my goal

_____
_____
_____

Daily Habits Checklist  ⊙ ⊙ ⊙ ⊙ ⊙

*I am adorable*

---

# Wednesday

I am _____

_____
_____
_____
_____
_____

Today I am GRATEFUL for

_____
_____
_____
_____
_____
_____

Today's tasks towards my goal

_____
_____
_____

Daily Habits Checklist  ⊙ ⊙ ⊙ ⊙ ⊙

*I am in the flow*

# Thursday

I am _____

_____
_____
_____
_____
_____

Today's tasks towards my goal

_____
_____
_____

Daily Habits Checklist  ⊙ ⊙ ⊙ ⊙ ⊙

Today I am GRATEFUL for _____

_____
_____
_____
_____
_____
_____
_____
_____

*I am*

---

# Friday

I am _____

_____
_____
_____
_____
_____

Today's tasks towards my goal

_____
_____
_____

Daily Habits Checklist  ⊙ ⊙ ⊙ ⊙ ⊙

Today I am GRATEFUL for _____

_____
_____
_____
_____
_____
_____
_____
_____

*I am health*

# Saturday

I am _____

_____
_____
_____
_____
_____

Today's tasks towards my goal

_____
_____
_____

Daily Habits Checklist  ⊙ ⊙ ⊙ ⊙ ⊙

Today I am GRATEFUL for

_____
_____
_____
_____
_____
_____
_____
_____

*I am grateful*

---

# Sunday Reflection

I am GRATEFUL for

_____
_____
_____

What was successful about this week?

_____
_____
_____

What will I do differently?

_____
_____
_____

Thoughts about my daily activities

⊙ _____
⊙ _____
⊙ _____
⊙ _____
⊙ _____

*I am fortunate*

# New week. *New goals.*

**Week Start Date** ☐

This week's daily habits

- *Heart* _____
- *Head* _____
- *Health* _____
- *Relationships* _____
- *Mission* _____

_____

**Goals for this week**
_____
_____
_____

**What is my 'WHY'**
_____
_____
_____

## Monday

I am _____
_____
_____
_____
_____
_____

Today's tasks towards my goal
_____
_____
_____

Daily Habits Checklist 🏆 🧠 🧘 👫 🚀

Today I am GRATEFUL for
_____
_____
_____
_____
_____
_____
_____
_____

*I am Brave*

# Tuesday

I am

Today I am GRATEFUL for

Today's tasks towards my goal

Daily Habits Checklist

*I am genuine*

---

# Wednesday

I am

Today I am GRATEFUL for

Today's tasks towards my goal

Daily Habits Checklist

*I am assertive*

## Thursday

I am _____

_____
_____
_____
_____
_____
_____

Today's tasks towards my goal

_____
_____
_____

Daily Habits Checklist  ⊙ ⊙ ⊙ ⊙ ⊙

Today I am GRATEFUL for

_____
_____
_____
_____
_____
_____
_____
_____

*I am healed*

---

## Friday

I am _____

_____
_____
_____
_____
_____
_____

Today's tasks towards my goal

_____
_____
_____

Daily Habits Checklist  ⊙ ⊙ ⊙ ⊙ ⊙

Today I am GRATEFUL for

_____
_____
_____
_____
_____
_____
_____
_____

*I am bold*

# Saturday

I am _____

_____
_____
_____
_____
_____

Today's tasks towards my goal

_____
_____
_____

Daily Habits Checklist  ⊙ ⊙ ⊙ ⊙ ⊙

Today I am GRATEFUL for

_____
_____
_____
_____
_____
_____
_____
_____

*I am strong*

---

# Sunday Reflection

I am GRATEFUL for

_____
_____

What was successful about this week?

_____
_____

What will I do differently?

_____
_____

Thoughts about my daily activities

⊙ _____
⊙ _____
⊙ _____
⊙ _____
⊙ _____

*I am love*

Month

# Remember why you started...

## Monthly Goal 1

_____
_____
_____
_____
_____
_____
_____
_____
_____
_____

## Monthly Goal 2

_____
_____
_____
_____
_____
_____
_____
_____
_____
_____

## Monthly Goal 3

_____
_____
_____
_____
_____
_____
_____
_____
_____
_____

## How I will celebrate

_____
_____
_____
_____
_____
_____
_____
_____
_____
_____

# VISION BOARD
Create your vision for the month

**Be** — who do you want to be?

**Do** — what do you want to do?

**Have** — what do you want to have?

**By the end of this month I will...** *(write in the present tense)*

_____
_____
_____
_____
_____
_____
_____
_____
_____
_____
_____

# New week. *New goals.*

Week Start Date

This week's daily habits

- *Heart* _____
- *Head* _____
- *Health* _____
- *Relationships* _____
- *Mission* _____

*Master the day. Then just keep doing that every day.*

Goals for this week
_____
_____
_____

What is my 'WHY'
_____
_____
_____

# Monday

I am
_____
_____
_____
_____
_____
_____

Today's tasks towards my goal
_____
_____
_____

Today I am GRATEFUL for
_____
_____
_____
_____
_____
_____
_____
_____
_____

Daily Habits Checklist

*I am graceful*

# Tuesday

I am _____

_____

_____

_____

_____

_____

_____

Today's tasks towards my goal

_____

_____

_____

Daily Habits Checklist  ⊛ ⊛ ⊛ ⊛ ⊛

Today I am GRATEFUL for

_____

_____

_____

_____

_____

_____

_____

_____

_____

_____

*I am brilliant*

---

# Wednesday

I am _____

_____

_____

_____

_____

_____

_____

Today's tasks towards my goal

_____

_____

_____

Daily Habits Checklist  ⊛ ⊛ ⊛ ⊛ ⊛

Today I am GRATEFUL for

_____

_____

_____

_____

_____

_____

_____

_____

_____

_____

*I am attractive*

## Thursday

I am _____
_____
_____
_____
_____
_____

Today's tasks towards my goal
_____
_____
_____

Daily Habits Checklist  ○ ○ ○ ○ ○

Today I am GRATEFUL for
_____
_____
_____
_____
_____
_____
_____
_____
_____

*I am generous*

## Friday

I am _____
_____
_____
_____
_____
_____

Today's tasks towards my goal
_____
_____
_____

Daily Habits Checklist  ○ ○ ○ ○ ○

Today I am GRATEFUL for
_____
_____
_____
_____
_____
_____
_____
_____
_____

*I am lively*

# Saturday

I am
_____
_____
_____
_____
_____
_____

Today's tasks towards my goal
_____
_____
_____

Daily Habits Checklist

Today I am GRATEFUL for
_____
_____
_____
_____
_____
_____
_____
_____
_____

*I am a teacher*

---

# Sunday Reflection

I am GRATEFUL for
_____
_____
_____

What was successful about this week?
_____
_____
_____

What will I do differently?
_____
_____
_____

Thoughts about my daily activities
_____
_____
_____
_____
_____

*I am spirited*

# New week. *New goals.*

Week Start Date

This week's daily habits

- *Heart* _____
- *Head* _____
- *Health* _____
- *Relationships* _____
- *Mission* _____

Goals for this week
_____
_____
_____

What is my 'WHY'
_____
_____
_____

## Monday

I am
_____
_____
_____
_____
_____
_____

Today's tasks towards my goal
_____
_____

Today I am GRATEFUL for
_____
_____
_____
_____
_____
_____
_____
_____
_____

Daily Habits Checklist

*I am loving*

# Tuesday

I am _____

_____

_____

_____

_____

Today's tasks towards my goal

_____

_____

Daily Habits Checklist  ⊙ ⊙ ⊙ ⊙ ⊙

Today I am GRATEFUL for _____

_____

_____

_____

_____

_____

_____

*I am masterful*

---

# Wednesday

I am _____

_____

_____

_____

_____

Today's tasks towards my goal

_____

_____

Daily Habits Checklist  ⊙ ⊙ ⊙ ⊙ ⊙

Today I am GRATEFUL for _____

_____

_____

_____

_____

_____

_____

*I am affluent*

# Thursday

I am _____
_____
_____
_____
_____
_____
_____ *I'm so proud of you.*

Today's tasks towards my goal
_____
_____
_____

Daily Habits Checklist  ⊙ ⊙ ⊙ ⊙ ⊙

Today I am GRATEFUL for
_____
_____
_____
_____
_____
_____
_____
_____
_____
_____

*I am bright*

---

# Friday

I am _____
_____
_____
_____
_____
_____
_____

Today's tasks towards my goal
_____
_____
_____

Daily Habits Checklist  ⊙ ⊙ ⊙ ⊙ ⊙

Today I am GRATEFUL for
_____
_____
_____
_____
_____
_____
_____
_____
_____
_____

*I am fulfilled*

# Saturday

I am _____

_____
_____
_____
_____
_____
_____

Today's tasks towards my goal

_____
_____
_____

Daily Habits Checklist  ⊛ ⊛ ⊛ ⊛ ⊛

Today I am GRATEFUL for

_____
_____
_____
_____
_____
_____
_____
_____
_____
_____

*I am happy*

---

# Sunday Reflection

I am GRATEFUL for

_____
_____
_____

What was successful about this week?

_____
_____

What will I do differently?

_____
_____
_____

Thoughts about my daily activities

⊛ _____
⊛ _____
⊛ _____
⊛ _____
⊛ _____

*I am free*

# New week. *New goals.*

Week Start Date

This week's daily habits

- Heart _____
- Head _____
- Health _____
- Relationships _____
- Mission _____

Goals for this week
_____
_____
_____

What is my 'WHY'
_____
_____
_____

## Monday

I am
_____
_____
_____
_____
_____
_____
_____

Today's tasks towards my goal
_____
_____
_____

Today I am GRATEFUL for
_____
_____
_____
_____
_____
_____
_____
_____
_____
_____

Daily Habits Checklist

*I am bighearted*

# Tuesday

I am _____

_____

_____

_____

_____

_____

Today's tasks towards my goal

_____

_____

_____

Daily Habits Checklist  ⊙ ⊙ ⊙ ⊙ ⊙

Today I am GRATEFUL for _____

_____

_____

_____

_____

_____

_____

_____

_____

*I am gorgeous*

---

# Wednesday

I am _____

_____

_____

_____

_____

_____

Today's tasks towards my goal

_____

_____

_____

Daily Habits Checklist  ⊙ ⊙ ⊙ ⊙ ⊙

Today I am GRATEFUL for _____

_____

_____

_____

_____

_____

_____

_____

_____

*I am authentic*

# Thursday

I am _____
_____
_____
_____
_____
_____

Today's tasks towards my goal
_____
_____
_____

Daily Habits Checklist  ⊙ ⊙ ⊙ ⊙ ⊙

Today I am GRATEFUL for
_____
_____
_____
_____
_____
_____
_____
_____

*I am magical*

---

# Friday

I am _____
_____
_____
_____
_____
_____

Today's tasks towards my goal
_____
_____
_____

Daily Habits Checklist  ⊙ ⊙ ⊙ ⊙ ⊙

Today I am GRATEFUL for
_____
_____
_____
_____
_____
_____
_____
_____

*I am abundant*

# Saturday

I am _____

_____

_____

_____

_____

_____

Today's tasks towards my goal

_____

_____

_____

Daily Habits Checklist  ⊛  ◉  ⊠  ⊛  ⊛

Today I am GRATEFUL for _____

_____

_____

_____

_____

_____

_____

_____

_____

*I am blessed*

---

# Sunday Reflection

I am GRATEFUL for

_____

_____

What was successful about this week?

_____

_____

What will I do differently?

_____

_____

*It doesn't matter how slow you go - just don't stop.*

Thoughts about my daily activities

⊛ _____

◉ _____

⊠ _____

⊛ _____

⊛ _____

*I am financially savy*

# New week. *New goals.*

Week Start Date ☐

This week's daily habits

- ♡ *Heart* _____
- 🧠 *Head* _____
- 🏋 *Health* _____
- 👥 *Relationships* _____
- 🚀 *Mission* _____

_____

Goals for this week
_____
_____
_____

What is my 'WHY'
_____
_____

*There will never be the perfect time to do a great thing.*

## Monday

I am
_____
_____
_____
_____
_____
_____
_____

Today's tasks towards my goal
_____
_____

Today I am GRATEFUL for
_____
_____
_____
_____
_____
_____
_____
_____
_____

Daily Habits Checklist ♡ 🧠 🏋 👥 🚀      *I am fit*

# Tuesday

I am _____

_____

_____

_____

_____

_____

Today's tasks towards my goal

_____

_____

_____

Daily Habits Checklist  ⓐ ⓑ ⓒ ⓓ ⓔ

Today I am GRATEFUL for

_____

_____

_____

_____

_____

_____

_____

_____

_____

*I am loyal*

---

# Wednesday

I am _____

_____

_____

_____

_____

_____

Today's tasks towards my goal

_____

_____

_____

Daily Habits Checklist  ⓐ ⓑ ⓒ ⓓ ⓔ

Today I am GRATEFUL for

_____

_____

_____

_____

_____

_____

_____

_____

_____

*I am adored*

# Thursday

I am _____

_____
_____
_____
_____
_____
_____

Today's tasks towards my goal

_____
_____
_____

Daily Habits Checklist

Today I am GRATEFUL for

_____
_____
_____
_____
_____
_____
_____
_____
_____

*I am successful*

---

# Friday

I am _____

_____
_____
_____
_____
_____
_____

Today's tasks towards my goal

_____
_____
_____

Daily Habits Checklist

Today I am GRATEFUL for

_____
_____
_____
_____
_____
_____
_____
_____
_____

*I am thankful*

# Saturday

I am _____

_____

_____

_____

_____

_____

_____

Today's tasks towards my goal

_____

_____

_____

Daily Habits Checklist  ⊙ ⊙ ⊙ ⊙ ⊙

Today I am GRATEFUL for _____

_____

_____

_____

_____

_____

_____

_____

_____

_____

_____

*I am feminine*

---

# Sunday Reflection

I am GRATEFUL for

_____

_____

_____

What was successful about this week?

_____

_____

_____

What will I do differently?

_____

_____

_____

Thoughts about my daily activities

⊙ _____

_____

⊙ _____

_____

⊙ _____

_____

⊙ _____

_____

⊙ _____

_____

*I am a money magnet*

# New week. *New goals.*

Week Start Date _____

This week's daily habits

- *Heart* _____
- *Head* _____
- *Health* _____
- *Relationships* _____
- *Mission* _____

Goals for this week
_____
_____
_____

What is my 'WHY'
_____
_____
_____

## Monday

I am _____
_____
_____
_____
_____
_____
_____

Today's tasks towards my goal
_____
_____
_____

Daily Habits Checklist

Today I am GRATEFUL for
_____
_____
_____
_____
_____
_____
_____
_____
_____

*I am active*

# Tuesday

I am _____

_____
_____
_____
_____
_____

Today's tasks towards my goal

_____
_____

Daily Habits Checklist  ⓢ ⓟ ⓐ ⓡ ⓡ

Today I am GRATEFUL for _____

_____
_____
_____
_____
_____
_____
_____

*I am a millionaire*

---

# Wednesday

I am _____

_____
_____
_____
_____
_____

Today's tasks towards my goal

_____
_____

Daily Habits Checklist  ⓢ ⓟ ⓐ ⓡ ⓡ

Today I am GRATEFUL for _____

_____
_____
_____
_____
_____
_____
_____

*I am calm*

# Thursday

I am _____

_____
_____
_____
_____
_____
_____

Today's tasks towards my goal

_____
_____
_____

Daily Habits Checklist  ⊕ ⊕ ⊕ ⊕ ⊕

Today I am GRATEFUL for

_____
_____
_____
_____
_____
_____
_____
_____

*I am inventive*

---

# Friday

I am _____

_____
_____
_____
_____
_____
_____

Today's tasks towards my goal

_____
_____
_____

Daily Habits Checklist  ⊕ ⊕ ⊕ ⊕ ⊕

Today I am GRATEFUL for

_____
_____
_____
_____
_____
_____
_____
_____

*I am youthful*

# Saturday

I am _____

_____
_____
_____
_____
_____
_____

Today's tasks towards my goal

*Keep going!*

_____
_____
_____

Daily Habits Checklist  ⊙ ⊙ ⊙ ⊙ ⊙

Today I am GRATEFUL for
_____
_____
_____
_____
_____
_____
_____
_____
_____

*I am independent*

---

# Sunday Reflection

I am GRATEFUL for
_____
_____
_____

What was successful about this week?
_____
_____
_____

What will I do differently?
_____
_____
_____

Thoughts about my daily activities

⊙ _____
⊙ _____
⊙ _____
⊙ _____
⊙ _____

*I am worthy*

Month 

# Half way...

## Monthly Goal 1

_____
_____
_____
_____
_____
_____
_____
_____
_____
_____

## Monthly Goal 2

_____
_____
_____
_____
_____
_____
_____
_____
_____
_____

## Monthly Goal 3

_____
_____
_____
_____
_____
_____
_____
_____
_____
_____

## How I will celebrate

_____
_____
_____
_____
_____
_____
_____
_____
_____
_____

# VISION BOARD
Create your vision for the month

**Be**
who do you want to be?

**Do**
what do you want to do?

**Have**
what do you want to have?

**By the end of this month I will...** *(write in the present tense)*

_____
_____
_____
_____
_____
_____
_____
_____
_____

# New week. *New goals.*

**Week Start Date** _____

This week's daily habits

- *Heart* _____
- *Head* _____
- *Health* _____
- *Relationships* _____
- *Mission* _____

*Everything you need to accomplish your goals is already in you.*

**Goals for this week**
_____
_____
_____

**What is my 'WHY'**
_____
_____
_____

## Monday

I am _____

_____
_____
_____
_____
_____

Today's tasks towards my goal
_____
_____
_____

**Today I am GRATEFUL for**
_____
_____
_____
_____
_____
_____

Daily Habits Checklist

*I am complete*

# Tuesday

I am _____

_____

_____

_____

_____

_____

Today's tasks towards my goal

_____

_____

Daily Habits Checklist  ⊛ ⊛ ⊛ ⊛ ⊛

Today I am GRATEFUL for _____

_____

_____

_____

_____

_____

_____

_____

*I am driven*

---

# Wednesday

I am _____

_____

_____

_____

_____

_____

Today's tasks towards my goal

_____

_____

Daily Habits Checklist  ⊛ ⊛ ⊛ ⊛ ⊛

Today I am GRATEFUL for _____

_____

_____

_____

_____

_____

_____

_____

*I am creative*

# Thursday

I am _____

_____

_____

_____

_____

_____

Today's tasks towards my goal

_____

_____

Daily Habits Checklist  ⊕ ⊕ ⊕ ⊕ ⊕

Today I am GRATEFUL for

_____

_____

_____

_____

_____

_____

_____

_____

*I am clear*

---

# Friday

I am _____

_____

_____

_____

_____

_____

Today's tasks towards my goal

_____

_____

Daily Habits Checklist  ⊕ ⊕ ⊕ ⊕ ⊕

Today I am GRATEFUL for

_____

_____

_____

_____

_____

_____

_____

_____

*I am connected*

# Saturday

I am _____

_____
_____
_____
_____
_____
_____

Today's tasks towards my goal

_____
_____
_____

Daily Habits Checklist  (○) (○) (○) (○) (○)

Today I am GRATEFUL for

_____
_____
_____
_____
_____
_____
_____
_____
_____
_____

*I am joy*

---

# Sunday Reflection

I am GRATEFUL for

_____
_____

What was successful about this week?

_____
_____

What will I do differently?

_____
_____
_____

Thoughts about my daily activities

(○) _____
(○) _____
(○) _____
(○) _____
(○) _____

*I am incredible*

# New week. *New goals.*

Week Start Date

This week's daily habits

- *Heart* _____
- *Head* _____
- *Health* _____
- *Relationships* _____
- *Mission* _____

Goals for this week
_____
_____
_____

What is my 'WHY'
_____
_____
_____

## Monday

I am
_____
_____
_____
_____
_____
_____

Today's tasks towards my goal
_____
_____
_____

Today I am GRATEFUL for
_____
_____
_____
_____
_____
_____
_____
_____

Daily Habits Checklist

*I am charming*

# Tuesday

I am _____

_____

_____

_____

_____

_____

Today's tasks towards my goal

_____

_____

Daily Habits Checklist ⓐ ⓑ ⓒ ⓓ ⓔ

Today I am GRATEFUL for _____

_____

_____

_____

_____

_____

_____

_____

*I am effervescent*

---

# Wednesday

I am _____

_____

_____

_____

_____

_____

Today's tasks towards my goal

_____

_____

Daily Habits Checklist ⓐ ⓑ ⓒ ⓓ ⓔ

Today I am GRATEFUL for _____

_____

_____

_____

_____

_____

_____

_____

*I am intuitive*

# Thursday

I am _____

_____

_____

_____

_____

_____

Today's tasks towards my goal

_____

_____

Daily Habits Checklist  ⓐ ⓑ ⓒ ⓓ ⓔ

Today I am GRATEFUL for
_____

_____

_____

_____

_____

_____

_____

_____

*I am enough*

---

# Friday

I am _____

_____

_____

_____

_____

_____

*Be gentle with yourself. You're doing the best you can!*

Today's tasks towards my goal

_____

_____

Daily Habits Checklist  ⓐ ⓑ ⓒ ⓓ ⓔ

Today I am GRATEFUL for
_____

_____

_____

_____

_____

_____

_____

_____

*I am innovative*

# Saturday

I am _____

_____
_____
_____
_____
_____

Today's tasks towards my goal

_____
_____
_____
_____

Daily Habits Checklist  ⊙ ⊙ ⊙ ⊙ ⊙

Today I am GRATEFUL for _____

_____
_____
_____
_____
_____
_____
_____
_____
_____

*I am confident*

---

# Sunday Reflection

I am GRATEFUL for

_____
_____

What was successful about this week?

_____
_____

What will I do differently?

_____
_____
_____

Thoughts about my daily activities

⊙ _____

⊙ _____

⊙ _____

⊙ _____

⊙ _____

*I am an inspiration*

# New week. *New goals.*

Week Start Date

This week's daily habits

- Heart _____
- Head _____
- Health _____
- Relationships _____
- Mission _____

Goals for this week
_____
_____
_____

What is my 'WHY'
_____
_____
_____

## Monday

I am _____
_____
_____
_____
_____
_____

Today's tasks towards my goal
_____
_____
_____

Today I am GRATEFUL for
_____
_____
_____
_____
_____
_____
_____

Daily Habits Checklist

*I am hilarious*

# Tuesday

I am _____

_____
_____
_____
_____
_____
_____

Today's tasks towards my goal

_____
_____
_____

Daily Habits Checklist  ⊕ ⊕ ⊕ ⊕ ⊕

Today I am GRATEFUL for
_____
_____
_____
_____
_____
_____
_____
_____
_____
_____

*I am honest*

---

# Wednesday

I am _____

_____
_____
_____
_____
_____
_____

Today's tasks towards my goal

_____
_____
_____

Daily Habits Checklist  ⊕ ⊕ ⊕ ⊕ ⊕

Today I am GRATEFUL for
_____
_____
_____
_____
_____
_____
_____
_____
_____
_____

*I am certain*

# Thursday

I am _____

_____
_____
_____
_____
_____

Today's tasks towards my goal

_____
_____

Daily Habits Checklist  ⊙ ⊙ ⊙ ⊙ ⊙

Today I am GRATEFUL for

_____
_____
_____
_____
_____
_____
_____

*I am wealthy*

---

# Friday

I am _____

_____
_____
_____
_____
_____

Today's tasks towards my goal

_____
_____

Daily Habits Checklist  ⊙ ⊙ ⊙ ⊙ ⊙

Today I am GRATEFUL for

_____
_____
_____
_____
_____
_____
_____

*I am powerful*

# Saturday

I am _____

_____

_____

_____

_____

_____

Today's tasks towards my goal

_____

_____

_____

Daily Habits Checklist

Today I am GRATEFUL for

_____

_____

_____

_____

_____

_____

_____

_____

*I am inspired*

---

# Sunday Reflection

I am GRATEFUL for

_____

_____

What was successful about this week?

_____

_____

What will I do differently?

_____

_____

Thoughts about my daily activities

_____

_____

_____

_____

_____

*I am peaceful*

# New week. New goals.

**Week Start Date**

This week's daily habits

- Heart _____
- Head _____
- Health _____
- Relationships _____
- Mission _____

**Goals for this week**
_____
_____
_____

**What is my 'WHY'**
_____
_____
_____

## Monday

I am _____
_____
_____
_____
_____

Today's tasks towards my goal
_____
_____
_____

Daily Habits Checklist

Today I am GRATEFUL for
_____
_____
_____
_____
_____
_____
_____

*I am kind*

# Tuesday

I am ____

Today I am GRATEFUL for ____

*You just can't beat the person who never gives up*

Today's tasks towards my goal

Daily Habits Checklist

*I am intelligent*

# Wednesday

I am ____

Today I am GRATEFUL for ____

Today's tasks towards my goal

Daily Habits Checklist

*I am courageous*

# Thursday

I am _____

_____
_____
_____
_____
_____

Today's tasks towards my goal

_____
_____
_____

Daily Habits Checklist  ⊙ ⊙ ⊙ ⊙ ⊙

Today I am GRATEFUL for

_____
_____
_____
_____
_____
_____
_____
_____

*I am imaginative*

---

# Friday

I am _____

_____
_____
_____
_____
_____

Today's tasks towards my goal

_____
_____
_____

Daily Habits Checklist  ⊙ ⊙ ⊙ ⊙ ⊙

Today I am GRATEFUL for

_____
_____
_____
_____
_____
_____
_____
_____

*I am wonderful*

# Saturday

I am _____

_____
_____
_____
_____
_____

Today's tasks towards my goal

_____
_____
_____

Daily Habits Checklist  ⊙ ⊙ ⊙ ⊙ ⊙

Today I am GRATEFUL for

_____
_____
_____
_____
_____
_____
_____
_____

*I am dedicated*

---

# Sunday Reflection

I am GRATEFUL for

_____
_____

What was successful about this week?

_____
_____

What will I do differently?

_____
_____

Thoughts about my daily activities

⊙ _____

⊙ _____

⊙ _____

⊙ _____

⊙ _____

*I am prosperous*

Month

# Your best month starts now...

## Monthly Goal 1

## Monthly Goal 2

## Monthly Goal 3

## How I will celebrate

# VISION BOARD
Create your vision for the month

**Be** — who do you want to be?

**Do** — what do you want to do?

**Have** — what do you want to have?

**By the end of this month I will...** *(write in the present tense)*

___
___
___
___
___
___
___
___
___
___
___

# New week. *New goals.*

**Week Start Date** _____

This week's daily habits

- *Heart* _____
- *Head* _____
- *Health* _____
- *Relationships* _____
- *Mission* _____

*Either you run the day or the day runs you - Jim Rohn*

Goals for this week
_____
_____
_____

What is my 'WHY'
_____
_____
_____

## Monday

I am _____
_____
_____
_____
_____
_____

Today's tasks towards my goal
_____
_____
_____

Today I am GRATEFUL for
_____
_____
_____
_____
_____
_____
_____
_____
_____

Daily Habits Checklist

*I am loved*

# Tuesday

I am _____

_____

_____

_____

_____

_____

Today's tasks towards my goal

_____

_____

Daily Habits Checklist  ⊛ ⊛ ⊛ ⊛ ⊛

Today I am GRATEFUL for _____

_____

_____

_____

_____

_____

_____

_____

*I am fearless*

---

# Wednesday

I am _____

_____

_____

_____

_____

_____

Today's tasks towards my goal

_____

_____

Daily Habits Checklist  ⊛ ⊛ ⊛ ⊛ ⊛

Today I am GRATEFUL for _____

_____

_____

_____

_____

_____

_____

_____

*I am me*

# Thursday

I am _____

_____

_____

_____

_____

_____

Today's tasks towards my goal

_____

_____

Daily Habits Checklist  ⊙ ⊙ ⊙ ⊙ ⊙

Today I am GRATEFUL for _____

_____

_____

_____

_____

_____

_____

_____

*I am helpful*

---

# Friday

I am _____

_____

_____

_____

_____

_____

Today's tasks towards my goal

_____

_____

Daily Habits Checklist  ⊙ ⊙ ⊙ ⊙ ⊙

Today I am GRATEFUL for _____

_____

_____

_____

_____

_____

_____

_____

*I am daring*

## Saturday

I am _____
_____
_____
_____
_____
_____

Today's tasks towards my goal
_____
_____
_____

Daily Habits Checklist  ⓐ ⓑ ⓒ ⓓ ⓔ

Today I am GRATEFUL for
_____
_____
_____
_____
_____
_____
_____
_____
_____

*I am sensational*

---

## Sunday Reflection

I am GRATEFUL for
_____
_____

What was successful about this week?
_____
_____

What will I do differently?
_____
_____
_____

Thoughts about my daily activities

ⓐ _____
ⓑ _____
ⓒ _____
ⓓ _____
ⓔ _____

*I am enthusiastic*

# New week. *New goals.*

Week Start Date [ ]

This week's daily habits

- Heart _____
- Head _____
- Health _____
- Relationships _____
- Mission _____

Goals for this week
_____
_____
_____

What is my 'WHY'
_____
_____
_____

## Monday

I am
_____
_____
_____
_____
_____
_____
_____

Today's tasks towards my goal
_____
_____
_____

Daily Habits Checklist

Today I am GRATEFUL for
_____
_____
_____
_____
_____
_____
_____
_____
_____
_____

*I am curious*

## Tuesday

I am _____

_____
_____
_____
_____
_____

Today's tasks towards my goal

_____
_____
_____

Daily Habits Checklist  ⓐ ⓑ ⓒ ⓓ ⓔ

Today I am GRATEFUL for
_____
_____
_____
_____
_____
_____
_____
_____
_____

*I am eager*

---

## Wednesday

I am _____

_____
_____
_____
_____
_____

Today's tasks towards my goal

_____
_____
_____

Daily Habits Checklist  ⓐ ⓑ ⓒ ⓓ ⓔ

Today I am GRATEFUL for

*You are amazing!*
_____
_____
_____
_____
_____
_____
_____
_____

*I am famous*

# Thursday

I am _____

_____

_____

_____

_____

_____

Today's tasks towards my goal

_____

_____

Daily Habits Checklist  ⊙ ⊙ ⊙ ⊙ ⊙

Today I am
GRATEFUL for
_____

_____

_____

_____

_____

_____

_____

_____

*I am proud*

---

# Friday

I am _____

_____

_____

_____

_____

_____

Today's tasks towards my goal

_____

_____

Daily Habits Checklist  ⊙ ⊙ ⊙ ⊙ ⊙

Today I am
GRATEFUL for
_____

_____

_____

_____

_____

_____

_____

_____

*I am quirky*

# Saturday

I am _____

_____

_____

_____

_____

_____

Today's tasks towards my goal

_____

_____

_____

Daily Habits Checklist  ⊙ ⊙ ⊙ ⊙ ⊙

Today I am GRATEFUL for

_____

_____

_____

_____

_____

_____

_____

_____

*I am soulful*

---

# Sunday Reflection

I am GRATEFUL for

_____

_____

What was successful about this week?

_____

_____

What will I do differently?

_____

_____

_____

Thoughts about my daily activities

⊙ _____

⊙ _____

⊙ _____

⊙ _____

⊙ _____

*I am kick ass*

# New week. *New goals.*

**Week Start Date** ☐

This week's daily habits

- ❤️ *Heart* _____
- 🧠 *Head* _____
- 🏋️ *Health* _____
- 👫 *Relationships* _____
- 🚀 *Mission* _____

_____

**Goals for this week**

_____
_____
_____

**What is my 'WHY'**

_____
_____
_____

## Monday

I am _____
_____
_____
_____
_____
_____

Today's tasks towards my goal
_____
_____
_____

**Today I am GRATEFUL for**
_____
_____
_____
_____
_____
_____
_____
_____

Daily Habits Checklist  ❤️ 🧠 🏋️ 👫 🚀    *I am knowledgeable*

## Tuesday

I am _____

_____
_____
_____
_____
_____
_____

Today's tasks towards my goal

_____
_____
_____

Daily Habits Checklist  ◯ ◯ ◯ ◯ ◯

Today I am GRATEFUL for

_____
_____
_____
_____
_____
_____
_____
_____

*I am lazer focused*

---

## Wednesday

I am _____

_____
_____
_____
_____
_____
_____

Today's tasks towards my goal

_____
_____
_____

Daily Habits Checklist  ◯ ◯ ◯ ◯ ◯

Today I am GRATEFUL for

_____
_____
_____
_____
_____
_____
_____
_____

*I am a leader*

## Thursday

I am _____

_____

_____

_____

_____

*There's something in you that the world needs.*

Today's tasks towards my goal

_____

_____

Daily Habits Checklist  🧘 🧠 🏋 👥 🚀

| Today I am GRATEFUL for |
|---|
| _____ |
| _____ |
| _____ |
| _____ |
| _____ |
| _____ |
| _____ |

*I am valuable*

---

## Friday

I am _____

_____

_____

_____

_____

_____

Today's tasks towards my goal

_____

_____

Daily Habits Checklist  🧘 🧠 🏋 👥 🚀

| Today I am GRATEFUL for |
|---|
| _____ |
| _____ |
| _____ |
| _____ |
| _____ |
| _____ |
| _____ |

*I am tranquil*

# Saturday

I am _____

_____

_____

_____

_____

_____

Today's tasks towards my goal

_____

_____

_____

Daily Habits Checklist

Today I am GRATEFUL for

_____

_____

_____

_____

_____

_____

_____

_____

_____

*I am legendary*

---

# Sunday Reflection

I am GRATEFUL for

_____

_____

What was successful about this week?

_____

_____

What will I do differently?

_____

_____

Thoughts about my daily activities

_____

_____

_____

_____

_____

*I am thorough*

# New week. *New goals.*

**Week Start Date** [ ]

This week's daily habits

- *Heart* _____
- *Head* _____
- *Health* _____
- *Relationships* _____
- *Mission* _____

**Goals for this week**
_____
_____
_____

**What is my 'WHY'**
_____
_____

## Monday

I am _____
_____
_____
_____
_____
_____

Today's tasks towards my goal
_____
_____
_____

Daily Habits Checklist

**Today I am GRATEFUL for**
_____
_____
_____
_____
_____
_____
_____

*I am organized*

## Tuesday

I am _____

_____

_____

_____

_____

_____

Today's tasks towards my goal

_____

_____

Daily Habits Checklist  ◯ ◯ ◯ ◯ ◯

Today I am GRATEFUL for
_____

_____

_____

_____

_____

_____

_____

_____

_____

*I am optimistic*

---

## Wednesday

I am _____

_____

_____

_____

_____

_____

Today's tasks towards my goal

_____

_____

Daily Habits Checklist  ◯ ◯ ◯ ◯ ◯

Today I am GRATEFUL for
_____

_____

_____

_____

_____

_____

_____

_____

_____

*I am learning*

# Thursday

I am _____

_____

_____

_____

_____

_____

_____

Today's tasks towards my goal

_____

_____

_____

Daily Habits Checklist  ⊙ ⊙ ⊙ ⊙ ⊙

**Today I am GRATEFUL for**

_____

_____

_____

_____

_____

_____

_____

_____

_____

_____

*I am trusting*

---

# Friday

I am _____

_____

_____

_____

_____

_____

_____

Today's tasks towards my goal

_____

_____

_____

Daily Habits Checklist  ⊙ ⊙ ⊙ ⊙ ⊙

**Today I am GRATEFUL for**

_____

_____

_____

_____

_____

_____

_____

_____

_____

_____

*I am one of a kind*

# Saturday

I am _____

_____
_____
_____
_____
_____
_____

Today's tasks towards my goal

_____
_____
_____

Daily Habits Checklist ⊙ ⊙ ⊙ ⊙ ⊙

Today I am
GRATEFUL for
_____

_____
_____
_____
_____
_____
_____
_____
_____
_____

*I am whole*

---

# Sunday Reflection

I am GRATEFUL for

_____
_____

What was successful about this week?

_____

*Believe in yourself - you've got this!*

What will I do differently?

_____
_____
_____

Thoughts about
my daily activities

⊙ _____

⊙ _____

⊙ _____

⊙ _____

⊙ _____

*I am light*

Month

## Don't give up..

### Monthly Goal ①
_____
_____
_____
_____
_____
_____
_____
_____
_____
_____

### Monthly Goal ②
_____
_____
_____
_____
_____
_____
_____
_____
_____
_____

### Monthly Goal ③
_____
_____
_____
_____
_____
_____
_____
_____
_____
_____

### How I will celebrate
_____
_____
_____
_____
_____
_____
_____
_____
_____
_____

# VISION BOARD
Create your vision for the month

who do you want to be?

what do you want to do?

what do you want to have?

**By the end of this month I will...** *(write in the present tense)*

_____
_____
_____
_____
_____
_____
_____
_____
_____

# New week. *New goals.*

Week Start Date

This week's daily habits

- Heart _____
- Head _____
- Health _____
- Relationships _____
- Mission _____

Goals for this week
_____
_____
_____

What is my 'WHY'
_____
_____
_____

## Monday

I am _____
_____
_____
_____
_____
_____

Today's tasks towards my goal
_____
_____
_____

Daily Habits Checklist

Today I am GRATEFUL for
_____
_____
_____
_____
_____
_____
_____
_____
_____

*I am natural*

# Tuesday

I am _____

_____

_____

_____

_____

Today's tasks towards my goal

_____

_____

Daily Habits Checklist  ⊛ ⊛ ⊛ ⊛ ⊛

Today I am GRATEFUL for

_____

_____

_____

_____

_____

_____

_____

*I am open*

---

# Wednesday

I am _____

_____

_____

_____

_____

Today's tasks towards my goal

_____

_____

Daily Habits Checklist  ⊛ ⊛ ⊛ ⊛ ⊛

Today I am GRATEFUL for

_____

_____

_____

_____

_____

_____

_____

*I am upbeat*

# Thursday

I am _____

_____

_____

_____

_____

_____

Today's tasks towards my goal

_____

_____

_____

Daily Habits Checklist  ⊙ ⊙ ⊙ ⊙ ⊙

Today I am GRATEFUL for

_____

_____

_____

_____

_____

_____

_____

*I am vibrant*

---

# Friday

I am _____

_____

_____

_____

_____

_____

Today's tasks towards my goal

_____

_____

_____

Daily Habits Checklist  ⊙ ⊙ ⊙ ⊙ ⊙

Today I am GRATEFUL for

_____

_____

_____

_____

_____

_____

_____

*I am hope*

# Saturday

I am _____

_____

_____

_____

_____

_____

Today's tasks towards my goal

_____

_____

_____

Daily Habits Checklist  ⊕ ⊕ ⊕ ⊕ ⊕

Today I am GRATEFUL for

_____

_____

_____

_____

_____

_____

_____

_____

*I am quick*

---

# Sunday Reflection

I am GRATEFUL for

_____

_____

What was successful about this week?

_____

_____

What will I do differently?

_____

_____

Thoughts about my daily activities

⊕ _____

⊕ _____

⊕ _____

⊕ _____

⊕ _____

*I am pretty*

# New week. *New goals.*

**Week Start Date** ☐

This week's daily habits

- Heart _____
- Head _____
- Health _____
- Relationships _____
- Mission _____

Goals for this week
_____
_____
_____

What is my 'WHY'
_____
_____
_____

## Monday

I am _____
_____
_____
_____
_____
_____
_____

Today's tasks towards my goal
_____
_____
_____

Today I am GRATEFUL for
_____
_____
_____
_____
_____
_____
_____
_____
_____

Daily Habits Checklist ○ ○ ○ ○ ○

*I am ready*

## Tuesday

I am _____

_____

_____

_____

_____

_____

Today's tasks towards my goal

_____

_____

_____

Daily Habits Checklist  ⊙ ⊙ ⊙ ⊙ ⊙

Today I am GRATEFUL for

_____

_____

_____

_____

_____

_____

_____

_____

*I am poised*

---

## Wednesday

I am _____

_____

_____

_____

_____

_____

Today's tasks towards my goal

_____

_____

_____

Daily Habits Checklist  ⊙ ⊙ ⊙ ⊙ ⊙

Today I am GRATEFUL for

_____

_____

_____

_____

_____

_____

_____

_____

*I am safe*

# Thursday

I am _____

_____
_____
_____
_____
_____
_____

Today's tasks towards my goal

_____
_____
_____

Daily Habits Checklist ⊕ ⊕ ⊕ ⊕ ⊕

Today I am GRATEFUL for

_____
_____
_____
_____
_____
_____
_____
_____
_____

*I am productive*

---

# Friday

I am _____

_____
_____
_____
_____
_____

*You must believe it, before you can receive it.*

Today's tasks towards my goal

_____
_____
_____

Daily Habits Checklist ⊕ ⊕ ⊕ ⊕ ⊕

Today I am GRATEFUL for

_____
_____
_____
_____
_____
_____
_____
_____
_____

*I am spontaneous*

# Saturday

I am _____

_____

_____

_____

_____

_____

Today's tasks towards my goal

_____

_____

_____

Daily Habits Checklist  ⊛ ⊛ ⊛ ⊛ ⊛

Today I am GRATEFUL for _____

_____

_____

_____

_____

_____

_____

_____

_____

*I am respected*

---

# Sunday Reflection

I am GRATEFUL for

_____

_____

_____

What was successful about this week?

_____

_____

_____

What will I do differently?

_____

_____

_____

Thoughts about my daily activities

⊛ _____

⊛ _____

⊛ _____

⊛ _____

⊛ _____

*I am smart*

# New week. *New goals.*

Week Start Date ☐

This week's daily habits

- 🕯️ *Heart* _____
- 🧠 *Head* _____
- 🧘 *Health* _____
- 👫 *Relationships* _____
- 🚀 *Mission* _____

Goals for this week
_____
_____
_____

What is my 'WHY'
_____
_____
_____

## Monday

I am _____
_____
_____
_____
_____
_____

Today's tasks towards my goal
_____
_____
_____

Today I am GRATEFUL for
_____
_____
_____
_____
_____
_____
_____

Daily Habits Checklist 🕯️ 🧠 🧘 👫 🚀

*I am splendid*

# Tuesday

I am _____

_____

_____

_____

_____

_____

Today's tasks towards my goal

_____

_____

Daily Habits Checklist  ⊕ ⊕ ⊕ ⊕ ⊕

Today I am GRATEFUL for _____

_____

_____

_____

_____

_____

_____

_____

*I am resilient*

---

# Wednesday

I am _____

_____

_____

_____

_____

_____

Today's tasks towards my goal

_____

_____

Daily Habits Checklist  ⊕ ⊕ ⊕ ⊕ ⊕

Today I am GRATEFUL for _____

_____

_____

_____

_____

_____

_____

_____

*I am positive*

# Thursday

I am _____

_____
_____
_____
_____
_____

Today's tasks towards my goal

_____
_____

Daily Habits Checklist  ⊙ ⊙ ⊙ ⊙ ⊙

Today I am GRATEFUL for _____

_____
_____
_____
_____
_____
_____
_____
_____

*I am willing*

---

# Friday

I am _____

_____
_____
_____
_____
_____

Today's tasks towards my goal

_____
_____

Daily Habits Checklist  ⊙ ⊙ ⊙ ⊙ ⊙

Today I am GRATEFUL for _____

_____
_____
_____
_____
_____
_____
_____
_____

*I am wise*

# Saturday

I am _____

_____
_____
_____
_____
_____
_____

Today's tasks towards my goal

_____
_____
_____

Daily Habits Checklist  ⊙ ⊙ ⊙ ⊙ ⊙

Today I am GRATEFUL for

_____
_____
_____
_____
_____
_____
_____

*I am shining*

---

# Sunday Reflection

I am GRATEFUL for

_____
_____
_____

What was successful about this week?

_____
_____
_____

What will I do differently?

_____
_____
_____

Thoughts about my daily activities

⊙ _____

⊙ _____

⊙ _____

⊙ _____

⊙ _____

*I am relaxed*

# New week. *New goals.*

Week Start Date _____

This week's daily habits

- 🧘 Heart _____
- 🧠 Head _____
- 🏋 Health _____
- 👨‍👩‍👧 Relationships _____
- 🚀 Mission _____

Goals for this week
_____
_____
_____

What is my 'WHY'
_____
_____
_____

## Monday

I am _____
_____
_____
_____
_____
_____

Today's tasks towards my goal
_____
_____
_____

Today I am GRATEFUL for
_____
_____
_____
_____
_____
_____
_____
_____

Daily Habits Checklist  🧘 🧠 🏋 👨‍👩‍👧 🚀

*I am a speaker*

## Tuesday

I am _____

_____

_____

_____

_____

Today's tasks towards my goal

_____

_____

_____

Daily Habits Checklist  ⓐ ⓑ ⓒ ⓓ ⓔ

Today I am GRATEFUL for _____

_____

_____

_____

_____

_____

_____

_____

*I am sexy*

---

## Wednesday

I am _____

_____

_____

_____

_____

Today's tasks towards my goal

_____

_____

_____

Daily Habits Checklist  ⓐ ⓑ ⓒ ⓓ ⓔ

Today I am GRATEFUL for _____

_____

_____

_____

_____

_____

_____

_____

*I am special*

# Thursday

I am _____

_____

_____

_____

_____

_____

Today's tasks towards my goal

_____

_____

_____

Daily Habits Checklist

Today I am GRATEFUL for

_____

_____

_____

_____

_____

_____

_____

_____

*I am blessed*

---

# Friday

I am _____

_____

_____

_____

_____

_____

Today's tasks towards my goal

_____

_____

_____

Daily Habits Checklist

Today I am GRATEFUL for

_____

_____

_____

_____

_____

_____

_____

_____

*I am happy*

# Saturday

I am _____

_____

_____

_____

_____

_____

Today's tasks towards my goal

_____

_____

_____

Daily Habits Checklist  ⊙ ⊙ ⊙ ⊙ ⊙

Today I am GRATEFUL for

_____

_____

_____

_____

_____

_____

_____

_____

_____

*I am hilarious*

---

# Sunday Reflection

I am GRATEFUL for

_____

_____

_____

What was successful about this week?

_____

_____

What will I do differently?

_____

_____

Thoughts about my daily activities

⊙ _____

⊙ _____

⊙ _____

⊙ _____

⊙ _____

*I am open*

# New week. *New goals.*

Week Start Date _____

This week's daily habits

- *Heart* _____
- *Head* _____
- *Health* _____
- *Relationships* _____
- *Mission* _____

*You must do the thing you think you cannot do - Eleanor Roosevelt*

Goals for this week
_____
_____
_____

What is my 'WHY'
_____
_____
_____

## Monday

I am _____
_____
_____
_____
_____
_____
_____

Today's tasks towards my goal
_____
_____
_____

Today I am GRATEFUL for
_____
_____
_____
_____
_____
_____
_____
_____
_____

Daily Habits Checklist

*I am sincere*

## Tuesday

I am _____

_____
_____
_____
_____
_____

Today's tasks towards my goal

_____
_____

Daily Habits Checklist  ⊙ ⊙ ⊙ ⊙ ⊙

Today I am GRATEFUL for

_____
_____
_____
_____
_____
_____
_____

*I am complete*

---

## Wednesday

I am _____

_____
_____
_____
_____
_____

Today's tasks towards my goal

_____
_____

Daily Habits Checklist  ⊙ ⊙ ⊙ ⊙ ⊙

Today I am GRATEFUL for

_____
_____
_____
_____
_____
_____
_____

*I am brilliant*

# Thursday
I am _____

_____
_____
_____
_____
_____
_____

Today's tasks towards my goal
_____
_____
_____

Daily Habits Checklist 🎂 🧠 🧘 👫 🚀

Today I am GRATEFUL for
_____
_____
_____
_____
_____
_____
_____
_____
_____

*I am incredible*

---

# Friday
I am _____

_____
_____
_____
_____
_____
_____

Today's tasks towards my goal
_____
_____
_____

Daily Habits Checklist 🎂 🧠 🧘 👫 🚀

Today I am GRATEFUL for
_____
_____
_____
_____
_____
_____
_____
_____
_____

*I am one of a kind*

# Saturday

I am _____

_____

_____

_____

_____

_____

Today's tasks towards my goal

_____

_____

_____

Daily Habits Checklist  ⊙ ⊙ ⊙ ⊙ ⊙

Today I am GRATEFUL for

_____

_____

_____

_____

_____

_____

_____

_____

*I am certain*

---

# Sunday Reflection

I am GRATEFUL for

_____

_____

What was successful about this week?

_____

_____

What will I do differently?

_____

_____

Thoughts about my daily activities

⊙ _____

⊙ _____

⊙ _____

⊙ _____

⊙ _____

*I am courageous*

Month

## Your best month starts now...

### Monthly Goal 1
_____
_____
_____
_____
_____
_____
_____
_____
_____

### Monthly Goal 2
_____
_____
_____
_____
_____
_____
_____
_____
_____

### Monthly Goal 3
_____
_____
_____
_____
_____
_____
_____
_____
_____

### How I will celebrate
_____
_____
_____
_____
_____
_____
_____
_____
_____

# VISION BOARD
Create your vision for the month

who do you want to be?

what do you want to do?

what do you want to have?

**By the end of this month I will...** *(write in the present tense)*

_____
_____
_____
_____
_____
_____
_____
_____
_____
_____
_____

# New week. *New goals.*

Week Start Date _____

This week's daily habits

- Heart _____
- Head _____
- Health _____
- Relationships _____
- Mission _____

Goals for this week
_____
_____
_____

What is my 'WHY'
_____
_____
_____

## Monday

I am _____
_____
_____
_____
_____
_____
_____

Today's tasks towards my goal
_____
_____
_____

Daily Habits Checklist

Today I am GRATEFUL for
_____
_____
_____
_____
_____
_____
_____
_____
_____

*I am helpful*

# Tuesday

I am _____

_____
_____
_____
_____
_____
_____

Today's tasks towards my goal

_____
_____
_____

Daily Habits Checklist  ⊙ ⊙ ⊙ ⊙ ⊙

**Today I am GRATEFUL for**

_____
_____
_____
_____
_____
_____
_____
_____
_____

*I am honest*

---

# Wednesday

I am _____

_____
_____
_____
_____
_____
_____

Today's tasks towards my goal

_____
_____
_____

Daily Habits Checklist  ⊙ ⊙ ⊙ ⊙ ⊙

**Today I am GRATEFUL for**

_____
_____
_____
_____
_____
_____
_____
_____
_____

*I am confident*

## Thursday

I am _____

_____
_____
_____
_____
_____

Today's tasks towards my goal

_____
_____

Daily Habits Checklist  ⚪ ⚪ ⚪ ⚪ ⚪

Today I am GRATEFUL for

_____
_____
_____
_____
_____
_____
_____
_____

*I am gorgeous*

---

## Friday

I am _____

_____
_____
_____
_____
_____

Today's tasks towards my goal

_____
_____

Daily Habits Checklist  ⚪ ⚪ ⚪ ⚪ ⚪

Today I am GRATEFUL for

_____
_____
_____
_____
_____
_____
_____
_____

*I am optimistic*

# Saturday

I am _____

_____

_____

_____

_____

_____

Today's tasks towards my goal

_____

_____

_____

Daily Habits Checklist  ⊛ ⊛ ⊛ ⊛ ⊛

Today I am GRATEFUL for

_____

_____

_____

_____

_____

_____

_____

_____

*I am bold*

---

# Sunday Reflection

I am GRATEFUL for

_____

_____

What was successful about this week?

_____

_____

What will I do differently?

_____

_____

_____

Thoughts about my daily activities

⊛ _____

⊛ _____

⊛ _____

⊛ _____

⊛ _____

*I am healthy*

# New week. *New goals.*

Week Start Date

This week's daily habits

- *Heart* _____
- *Head* _____
- *Health* _____
- *Relationships* _____
- *Mission* _____

*You were made to do hard things. So believe in yourself.*

**Goals for this week**
_____
_____
_____

**What is my 'WHY'**
_____
_____
_____

## Monday

I am
_____
_____
_____
_____
_____
_____

Today's tasks towards my goal
_____
_____
_____

Today I am GRATEFUL for
_____
_____
_____
_____
_____
_____
_____
_____
_____

Daily Habits Checklist

*I am Brave*

# Tuesday

I am _____

_____
_____
_____
_____
_____
_____

Today's tasks towards my goal

_____
_____
_____

Daily Habits Checklist  ⊛ ⊛ ⊛ ⊛ ⊛

Today I am GRATEFUL for

_____
_____
_____
_____
_____
_____
_____
_____
_____

*I am imaginative*

---

# Wednesday

I am _____

_____
_____
_____
_____
_____
_____

Today's tasks towards my goal

_____
_____
_____

Daily Habits Checklist  ⊛ ⊛ ⊛ ⊛ ⊛

Today I am GRATEFUL for

_____
_____
_____
_____
_____
_____
_____
_____
_____

*I am connected*

# Thursday

I am _____

_____

_____

_____

_____

_____

Today's tasks towards my goal

_____

_____

Daily Habits Checklist  ⊙ ⊙ ⊙ ⊙ ⊙

Today I am GRATEFUL for

_____

_____

_____

_____

_____

_____

_____

_____

*I am organized*

---

# Friday

I am _____

_____

_____

_____

_____

_____

Today's tasks towards my goal

_____

_____

Daily Habits Checklist  ⊙ ⊙ ⊙ ⊙ ⊙

Today I am GRATEFUL for

_____

_____

_____

_____

_____

_____

_____

_____

*I am trusting*

# Saturday

I am _____

_____

_____

_____

_____

_____

Today's tasks towards my goal

_____

_____

_____

Daily Habits Checklist  ⊙ ⊙ ⊙ ⊙ ⊙

Today I am GRATEFUL for

_____

_____

_____

_____

_____

_____

_____

_____

*I am bighearted*

---

# Sunday Reflection

I am GRATEFUL for

_____

_____

_____

What was successful about this week?

_____

_____

What will I do differently?

_____

_____

_____

Thoughts about my daily activities

⊙ _____

⊙ _____

⊙ _____

⊙ _____

⊙ _____

*I am calm*

# New week. *New goals.*

Week Start Date

This week's daily habits

- *Heart* ___
- *Head* ___
- *Health* ___
- *Relationships* ___
- *Mission* ___

Goals for this week
___
___
___

What is my 'WHY'
___
___
___

## Monday

I am ___
___
___
___
___
___

Today's tasks towards my goal
___
___

Today I am GRATEFUL for
___
___
___
___
___
___
___

Daily Habits Checklist

*I am genuine*

# Tuesday

I am _____

_____

_____

_____

_____

_____

Today's tasks towards my goal

_____

_____

_____

Daily Habits Checklist  ⚪ ⚪ ⚪ ⚪ ⚪

Today I am GRATEFUL for _____

_____

_____

_____

_____

_____

_____

_____

*I am hope*

---

# Wednesday

I am _____

_____

_____

_____

_____

_____

Today's tasks towards my goal

_____

_____

_____

Daily Habits Checklist  ⚪ ⚪ ⚪ ⚪ ⚪

Today I am GRATEFUL for _____

_____

_____

_____

_____

_____

_____

_____

*I am powerful*

## Thursday

I am _____

_____

_____

_____

_____

Today's tasks towards my goal

_____

_____

_____

Daily Habits Checklist  ⊛ ⊛ ⊛ ⊛ ⊛

Today I am GRATEFUL for

_____

_____

_____

_____

_____

_____

_____

_____

*I am graceful*

---

## Friday

I am _____

_____

_____

_____

_____

Today's tasks towards my goal

_____

_____

_____

Daily Habits Checklist  ⊛ ⊛ ⊛ ⊛ ⊛

Today I am GRATEFUL for

_____

_____

_____

_____

_____

_____

_____

_____

*I am thorough*

# Saturday

I am _____

_____
_____
_____
_____
_____
_____

Today's tasks towards my goal

_____
_____
_____

Daily Habits Checklist  ⊙ ⊙ ⊙ ⊙ ⊙

Today I am GRATEFUL for

_____
_____
_____
_____
_____
_____
_____
_____
_____
_____

*I am grateful*

---

# Sunday Reflection

I am GRATEFUL for

_____
_____

What was successful about this week?

_____
_____

What will I do differently?

_____
_____

Thoughts about my daily activities

⊙ _____
⊙ _____
⊙ _____
⊙ _____
⊙ _____

*I am a money magnet*

# New week. *New goals.*

Week Start Date ☐

This week's daily habits

- Heart _____
- Head _____
- Health _____
- Relationships _____
- Mission _____

Goals for this week
_____
_____
_____

What is my 'WHY'
_____
_____
_____

## Monday

I am _____
_____
_____
_____
_____
_____
_____

Today's tasks towards my goal
_____
_____
_____

Today I am GRATEFUL for
_____
_____
_____
_____
_____
_____
_____
_____
_____
_____

Daily Habits Checklist

*I am eager*

# Tuesday

I am _____

_____

_____

_____

_____

_____

Today's tasks towards my goal

_____

_____

_____

Daily Habits Checklist  ⊙ ⊙ ⊙ ⊙ ⊙

Today I am GRATEFUL for

_____

_____

_____

_____

_____

_____

_____

_____

*I am a leader*

---

# Wednesday

I am _____

_____

_____

_____

_____

_____

Today's tasks towards my goal

_____

_____

_____

Daily Habits Checklist  ⊙ ⊙ ⊙ ⊙ ⊙

Today I am GRATEFUL for

_____

_____

_____

_____

_____

_____

_____

_____

*I am learning*

# Thursday

I am _____
_____
_____
_____
_____

Today's tasks towards my goal
_____
_____
_____

Daily Habits Checklist  ⊙ ⊙ ⊙ ⊙ ⊙

Today I am GRATEFUL for
_____
_____
_____
_____
_____
_____
_____
_____

*I am creative*

---

# Friday

I am _____
_____
_____
_____
_____

Today's tasks towards my goal
_____
_____
_____

Daily Habits Checklist  ⊙ ⊙ ⊙ ⊙ ⊙

Today I am GRATEFUL for
_____
_____
_____
_____
_____
_____
_____
_____

*I am charming*

# Saturday

I am _____

_____
_____
_____
_____
_____

Today's tasks towards my goal

_____
_____
_____

Daily Habits Checklist  ⊛ ⊛ ⊛ ⊛ ⊛

Today I am GRATEFUL for _____

_____
_____
_____
_____
_____
_____
_____

*I am enthusiastic*

---

# Sunday Reflection

I am GRATEFUL for

_____
_____

What was successful about this week?

_____
_____

What will I do differently?

_____
_____
_____

Thoughts about my daily activities

⊛ _____

⊛ _____

⊛ _____

⊛ _____

⊛ _____

*I am legendary*

Month ☐

# Keep going...

## Monthly Goal ①

_____
_____
_____
_____
_____
_____
_____
_____
_____

## Monthly Goal ②

_____
_____
_____
_____
_____
_____
_____
_____
_____

## Monthly Goal ③

_____
_____
_____
_____
_____
_____
_____
_____

## How I will celebrate

_____
_____
_____
_____
_____
_____
_____
_____

# VISION BOARD
Create your vision for the month

Be
who do you want to be?

Do
what do you want to do?

Have
what do you want to have?

**By the end of this month I will...** *(write in the present tense)*

___
___
___
___
___
___
___
___
___

# New week. *New goals.*

**Week Start Date** ☐

This week's daily habits

- *Heart* _____
- *Head* _____
- *Health* _____
- *Relationships* _____
- *Mission* _____

*You're allowed to scream, you're allowed to cry but do not give up.*

**Goals for this week**
_____
_____
_____

**What is my 'WHY'**
_____
_____
_____

## Monday

**I am**
_____
_____
_____
_____
_____
_____

**Today's tasks towards my goal**
_____
_____
_____

**Daily Habits Checklist** ⊙ ⊙ ⊙ ⊙ ⊙

**Today I am GRATEFUL for**
_____
_____
_____
_____
_____
_____
_____
_____

*I am curious*

# Tuesday

I am _____

_____
_____
_____
_____
_____

Today's tasks towards my goal

_____
_____
_____

Daily Habits Checklist ⭘ ⭘ ⭘ ⭘ ⭘

Today I am GRATEFUL for _____

_____
_____
_____
_____
_____
_____
_____
_____
_____

*I am dedicated*

---

# Wednesday

I am _____

_____
_____
_____
_____
_____

Today's tasks towards my goal

_____
_____
_____

Daily Habits Checklist ⭘ ⭘ ⭘ ⭘ ⭘

Today I am GRATEFUL for _____

_____
_____
_____
_____
_____
_____
_____
_____
_____

*I am a speaker*

# Thursday

I am _____

_____

_____

_____

_____

_____

_____

Today's tasks towards my goal

_____

_____

Daily Habits Checklist  ◯ ◯ ◯ ◯ ◯

Today I am GRATEFUL for

_____

_____

_____

_____

_____

_____

_____

_____

_____

*I am daring*

---

# Friday

I am _____

_____

_____

_____

_____

_____

_____

Today's tasks towards my goal

_____

_____

Daily Habits Checklist  ◯ ◯ ◯ ◯ ◯

Today I am GRATEFUL for

_____

_____

_____

_____

_____

_____

_____

_____

_____

*I am kind*

# Saturday

I am _____

_____
_____
_____
_____
_____

Today's tasks towards my goal

_____
_____
_____

Daily Habits Checklist ⚖ 🧠 🚶 👥 🚀

Today I am GRATEFUL for

_____
_____
_____
_____
_____
_____
_____
_____

*I am driven*

---

# Sunday Reflection

I am GRATEFUL for

_____
_____
_____

What was successful about this week?

_____
_____

What will I do differently?

_____
_____

Thoughts about my daily activities

⚖ _____

🧠 _____

🚶 _____

👥 _____

🚀 _____

*I am lazer focused*

# New week. *New goals.*

**Week Start Date**

This week's daily habits

- Heart _____
- Head _____
- Health _____
- Relationships _____
- Mission _____

_____

**Goals for this week**
_____
_____
_____

**What is my 'WHY'**
_____
_____
_____

# Monday

I am _____

_____

_____

_____

_____

_____

Today's tasks towards my goal
_____

_____

Daily Habits Checklist

**Today I am GRATEFUL for**
_____
_____
_____
_____
_____
_____
_____
_____

*I am effervescent*

# Tuesday

I am _____

_____
_____
_____
_____
_____
_____

Today's tasks towards my goal

_____
_____
_____

Daily Habits Checklist  ⊛ ⊛ ⊛ ⊛ ⊛

Today I am GRATEFUL for _____

_____
_____
_____
_____
_____
_____
_____
_____
_____
_____

*I am fearless*

---

# Wednesday

I am _____

_____
_____
_____
_____
_____
_____

Today's tasks towards my goal

_____
_____
_____

Daily Habits Checklist  ⊛ ⊛ ⊛ ⊛ ⊛

Today I am GRATEFUL for _____

_____
_____
_____
_____
_____
_____
_____
_____
_____
_____

*I am knowledgeable*

# Thursday

I am _____

_____

_____

_____

_____

Today's tasks towards my goal

_____

_____

Daily Habits Checklist  ⊘ ⊘ ⊘ ⊘ ⊘

Today I am GRATEFUL for

_____

_____

_____

_____

_____

_____

_____

*I am abundant*

---

# Friday

I am _____

_____

_____

_____

_____

Today's tasks towards my goal

_____

_____

Daily Habits Checklist  ⊘ ⊘ ⊘ ⊘ ⊘

Today I am GRATEFUL for

_____

_____

_____

_____

_____

_____

_____

*I am inspired*

# Saturday

I am _____

_____

_____

_____

_____

*How long should you try? Until - Jim Rohn*

Today's tasks towards my goal

_____

_____

_____

Daily Habits Checklist  ⊛ ⊛ ⊛ ⊛ ⊛

Today I am GRATEFUL for

_____

_____

_____

_____

_____

_____

_____

*I am adored*

---

# Sunday Reflection

I am GRATEFUL for

_____

_____

What was successful about this week?

_____

_____

What will I do differently?

_____

_____

Thoughts about my daily activities

⊛ _____

⊛ _____

⊛ _____

⊛ _____

⊛ _____

*I am beautiful*

# New week. *New goals.*

**Week Start Date** ☐

This week's daily habits

- *Heart* _____
- *Head* _____
- *Health* _____
- *Relationships* _____
- *Mission* _____

*Don't give up before the miracle happens~ Fannie Flag*

**Goals for this week**
_____
_____
_____

**What is my 'WHY'**
_____
_____
_____

# Monday

**I am**
_____
_____
_____
_____
_____

**Today's tasks towards my goal**
_____
_____
_____

Daily Habits Checklist ☐ ☐ ☐ ☐ ☐

**Today I am GRATEFUL for**
_____
_____
_____
_____
_____
_____
_____

*I am joy*

# Tuesday

I am _____

_____

_____

_____

_____

_____

Today's tasks towards my goal

_____

_____

Daily Habits Checklist  ⊙ ⊙ ⊙ ⊙ ⊙

Today I am GRATEFUL for

_____

_____

_____

_____

_____

_____

_____

_____

*I am intelligent*

---

# Wednesday

I am _____

_____

_____

_____

_____

_____

Today's tasks towards my goal

_____

_____

Daily Habits Checklist  ⊙ ⊙ ⊙ ⊙ ⊙

Today I am GRATEFUL for

_____

_____

_____

_____

_____

_____

_____

_____

*I am soulful*

# Thursday

I am

_____
_____
_____
_____
_____
_____

Today's tasks towards my goal

_____
_____
_____

Daily Habits Checklist  ⊘ ⊘ ⊘ ⊘ ⊘

Today I am GRATEFUL for

_____
_____
_____
_____
_____
_____
_____

*I am a teacher*

---

# Friday

I am

_____
_____
_____
_____
_____
_____

Today's tasks towards my goal

_____
_____
_____

Daily Habits Checklist  ⊘ ⊘ ⊘ ⊘ ⊘

Today I am GRATEFUL for

_____
_____
_____
_____
_____
_____
_____

*I am assertive*

# Saturday

I am _____

_____
_____
_____
_____
_____
_____

Today's tasks towards my goal

_____
_____
_____

Daily Habits Checklist  ⊙ ⊙ ⊙ ⊙ ⊙

Today I am GRATEFUL for

_____
_____
_____
_____
_____
_____
_____
_____
_____
_____

*I am love*

---

# Sunday Reflection

I am GRATEFUL for

_____
_____
_____

What was successful about this week?

_____
_____
_____

What will I do differently?

_____
_____
_____
_____

Thoughts about my daily activities

⊙ _____
⊙ _____
⊙ _____
⊙ _____
⊙ _____

*I am adorable*

though
# New week. *New goals.*

Week Start Date _____

This week's daily habits

- *Heart* _____
- *Head* _____
- *Health* _____
- *Relationships* _____
- *Mission* _____

**Goals for this week**
_____
_____
_____

**What is my 'WHY'**
_____
_____
_____

# Monday

I am
_____
_____
_____
_____
_____
_____

Today's tasks towards my goal
_____
_____
_____

Today I am GRATEFUL for
_____
_____
_____
_____
_____
_____
_____
_____

Daily Habits Checklist  ◯ ◯ ◯ ◯ ◯      *I am successful*

# Tuesday

I am _____

_____

_____

_____

_____

Today's tasks towards my goal

_____

_____

_____

Daily Habits Checklist  ⊙ ⊙ ⊙ ⊙ ⊙

Today I am GRATEFUL for

_____

_____

_____

_____

_____

_____

_____

*I am strong*

---

# Wednesday

I am _____

_____

_____

_____

_____

Today's tasks towards my goal

_____

_____

_____

Daily Habits Checklist  ⊙ ⊙ ⊙ ⊙ ⊙

Today I am GRATEFUL for

_____

_____

_____

_____

_____

_____

_____

*I am inventive*

# Thursday

I am _____

_____

_____

_____

_____

_____

Today's tasks towards my goal

_____

_____

Daily Habits Checklist  ⊙ ⊙ ⊙ ⊙ ⊙

Today I am GRATEFUL for

_____

_____

_____

_____

_____

_____

_____

_____

*I am authentic*

---

# Friday

I am _____

_____

_____

_____

_____

_____

Today's tasks towards my goal

_____

_____

Daily Habits Checklist  ⊙ ⊙ ⊙ ⊙ ⊙

Today I am GRATEFUL for

_____

_____

_____

_____

_____

_____

_____

_____

*I am kick ass*

# Saturday

I am _____

_____

_____

_____

_____

_____

Today's tasks towards my goal

_____

_____

_____

Daily Habits Checklist  ⊙ ⊙ ⊙ ⊙ ⊙

Today I am GRATEFUL for _____

_____

_____

_____

_____

_____

_____

_____

_____

*I am me*

---

# Sunday Reflection

I am GRATEFUL for

_____

_____

What was successful about this week?

_____

_____

What will I do differently?

_____

_____

Thoughts about my daily activities

⊙ _____

_____

⊙ _____

_____

⊙ _____

_____

⊙ _____

_____

⊙ _____

*I am financially savy*

Month ☐

# Last month... Finish strong...

## Monthly Goal 1

_____
_____
_____
_____
_____
_____
_____
_____

## Monthly Goal 2

_____
_____
_____
_____
_____
_____
_____
_____

## Monthly Goal 3

_____
_____
_____
_____
_____
_____
_____
_____

## How I will celebrate

_____
_____
_____
_____
_____
_____
_____
_____

# VISION BOARD
Create your vision for the month

**Be** — who do you want to be?

**Do** — what do you want to do?

**Have** — what do you want to have?

**By the end of this month I will...** *(write in the present tense)*

_____
_____
_____
_____
_____
_____
_____
_____
_____

# New week. *New goals.*

Week Start Date ☐

This week's daily habits

- *Heart* _____
- *Head* _____
- *Health* _____
- *Relationships* _____
- *Mission* _____

*Happy people plan actions, they don't plan results - Dennis Waitley*

Goals for this week
_____
_____
_____

What is my 'WHY'
_____
_____
_____

## Monday

I am
_____
_____
_____
_____
_____
_____

Today's tasks towards my goal
_____
_____
_____

Today I am GRATEFUL for
_____
_____
_____
_____
_____
_____
_____

Daily Habits Checklist

*I am a Badass*

## Tuesday

I am _____

_____

_____

_____

_____

_____

Today's tasks towards my goal

_____

_____

Daily Habits Checklist ⓐ ⓑ ⓒ ⓓ ⓔ

Today I am GRATEFUL for
_____

_____

_____

_____

_____

_____

_____

_____

*I am active*

---

## Wednesday

I am _____

_____

_____

_____

_____

_____

Today's tasks towards my goal

_____

_____

Daily Habits Checklist ⓐ ⓑ ⓒ ⓓ ⓔ

Today I am GRATEFUL for
_____

_____

_____

_____

_____

_____

_____

_____

*I am masterful*

# Thursday

I am _____

_____

_____

_____

_____

_____

Today's tasks towards my goal

_____

_____

_____

Daily Habits Checklist  ⊙ ⊙ ⊙ ⊙ ⊙

Today I am GRATEFUL for
_____

_____

_____

_____

_____

_____

_____

_____

_____

*I am in the flow*

---

# Friday

I am _____

_____

_____

_____

_____

_____

Today's tasks towards my goal

_____

_____

_____

Daily Habits Checklist  ⊙ ⊙ ⊙ ⊙ ⊙

Today I am GRATEFUL for
_____

_____

_____

_____

_____

_____

_____

_____

_____

*I am loving*

# Saturday

I am _____

Today I am GRATEFUL for
_____

Today's tasks towards my goal
_____

Daily Habits Checklist  ⊛ ⊛ ⊛ ⊛ ⊛

*I am famous*

---

# Sunday Reflection

I am GRATEFUL for
_____

What was successful about this week?
_____

What will I do differently?
_____

Thoughts about my daily activities
_____

*I am poised*

# New week. *New goals.*

Week Start Date _____

This week's daily habits

- *Heart* _____
- *Head* _____
- *Health* _____
- *Relationships* _____
- *Mission* _____

_____

Goals for this week
_____
_____
_____

What is my 'WHY'
_____
_____
_____

## Monday

I am _____
_____
_____
_____
_____
_____
_____

Today's tasks towards my goal
_____
_____
_____

Today I am GRATEFUL for
_____
_____
_____
_____
_____
_____
_____
_____
_____

Daily Habits Checklist

*I am attractive*

## Tuesday

I am ____

____
____
____
____
____
____

Today's tasks towards my goal

____
____
____

Daily Habits Checklist

Today I am GRATEFUL for

____
____
____
____
____
____
____
____
____

*I am magical*

---

## Wednesday

I am ____

____
____
____
____
____
____

Today's tasks towards my goal

____
____
____

Daily Habits Checklist

Today I am GRATEFUL for

____
____
____
____
____
____
____
____
____

*I am willing*

# Thursday

I am _____

_____

_____

_____

_____

_____

Today's tasks towards my goal

_____

_____

_____

Daily Habits Checklist  ⚪ ⚪ ⚪ ⚪ ⚪

Today I am GRATEFUL for _____

_____

_____

_____

_____

_____

_____

_____

_____

_____

*I am positive*

---

# Friday

I am _____

_____

_____

_____

_____

_____

Today's tasks towards my goal

_____

_____

_____

Daily Habits Checklist  ⚪ ⚪ ⚪ ⚪ ⚪

Today I am GRATEFUL for _____

_____

_____

_____

_____

_____

_____

_____

_____

_____

*I am loyal*

# Saturday

I am _____

_____

_____

_____

_____

_____

Today's tasks towards my goal

_____

_____

_____

Daily Habits Checklist  ⊙ ⊙ ⊙ ⊙ ⊙

Today I am GRATEFUL for

_____

_____

_____

_____

_____

_____

_____

*I am feminine*

---

# Sunday Reflection

I am GRATEFUL for

_____

_____

What was successful about this week?

_____

_____

What will I do differently?

_____

_____

Thoughts about my daily activities

⊙ _____

⊙ _____

⊙ _____

⊙ _____

⊙ _____

*I am enough*

# New week. *New goals.*

Week Start Date [ ]

This week's daily habits

- Heart _____
- Head _____
- Health _____
- Relationships _____
- Mission _____

*Finishing strong is the only respectable way to finish - Gary Ryan Blair*

Goals for this week
_____
_____
_____

What is my 'WHY'
_____
_____

## Monday

I am _____
_____
_____
_____
_____
_____

Today's tasks towards my goal
_____
_____
_____

Daily Habits Checklist

Today I am GRATEFUL for
_____
_____
_____
_____
_____
_____
_____

*I am a millionaire*

## Tuesday

I am _____

_____

_____

_____

_____

_____

Today's tasks towards my goal

_____

_____

Daily Habits Checklist

Today I am GRATEFUL for

_____

_____

_____

_____

_____

_____

_____

_____

*I am peaceful*

---

## Wednesday

I am _____

_____

_____

_____

_____

_____

_____

Today's tasks towards my goal

_____

_____

Daily Habits Checklist

Today I am GRATEFUL for

_____

_____

_____

_____

_____

_____

_____

_____

*I am wise*

# Thursday

I am _____

_____
_____
_____
_____
_____

Today's tasks towards my goal

_____
_____

Daily Habits Checklist  ⊙ ⊙ ⊙ ⊙ ⊙

Today I am GRATEFUL for

_____
_____
_____
_____
_____
_____
_____

*I am worthy*

---

# Friday

I am _____

_____
_____
_____
_____
_____

Today's tasks towards my goal

_____
_____

Daily Habits Checklist  ⊙ ⊙ ⊙ ⊙ ⊙

Today I am GRATEFUL for

_____
_____
_____
_____
_____
_____
_____

*I am wonderful*

# Saturday

I am _____

_____

_____

_____

_____

_____

Today's tasks towards my goal

_____

_____

_____

Daily Habits Checklist  ⊙ ⊙ ⊙ ⊙ ⊙

Today I am GRATEFUL for

_____

_____

_____

_____

_____

_____

_____

_____

*I am lively*

---

# Sunday Reflection

I am GRATEFUL for

_____

_____

What was successful about this week?

_____

_____

What will I do differently?

_____

_____

_____

Thoughts about my daily activities

⊙ _____

⊙ _____

⊙ _____

⊙ _____

⊙ _____

*I am upbeat*

# New week. *New goals.*

**Week Start Date** _____

This week's daily habits

- *Heart* _____
- *Head* _____
- *Health* _____
- *Relationships* _____
- *Mission* _____

Goals for this week
_____
_____
_____

What is my 'WHY'
_____
_____
_____

## Monday

I am
_____
_____
_____
_____
_____
_____

Today's tasks towards my goal
_____
_____
_____

Today I am GRATEFUL for
_____
_____
_____
_____
_____
_____
_____
_____

Daily Habits Checklist

*I am valuable*

## Tuesday

I am _____

_____
_____
_____
_____
_____
_____

Today's tasks towards my goal

_____
_____
_____

Daily Habits Checklist ⚪ ⚪ ⚪ ⚪ ⚪

Today I am GRATEFUL for

_____
_____
_____
_____
_____
_____
_____
_____

*I am wealthy*

---

## Wednesday

I am _____

_____
_____
_____
_____
_____
_____

Today's tasks towards my goal

_____
_____
_____

Daily Habits Checklist ⚪ ⚪ ⚪ ⚪ ⚪

Today I am GRATEFUL for

_____
_____
_____
_____
_____
_____
_____
_____

*I am youthful*

# Thursday

I am _____

_____

_____

_____

_____

_____

_____

Today's tasks towards my goal

_____

_____

Daily Habits Checklist  ◯ ◯ ◯ ◯ ◯

Today I am GRATEFUL for

_____

_____

_____

_____

_____

_____

_____

_____

*I am vibrant*

---

# Friday

I am _____

_____

_____

_____

_____

_____

_____

Today's tasks towards my goal

_____

_____

Daily Habits Checklist  ◯ ◯ ◯ ◯ ◯

Today I am GRATEFUL for

_____

_____

_____

_____

_____

_____

_____

_____

*I am respected*

# Saturday

I am _____

_____
_____
_____
_____
_____
_____

Today's tasks towards my goal

_____
_____
_____

Daily Habits Checklist  ⊛ ⊛ ⊛ ⊛ ⊛

Today I am GRATEFUL for

_____
_____
_____
_____
_____
_____
_____
_____

*I am fulfilled*

---

# Sunday Reflection

I am GRATEFUL for

_____
_____

What was successful about this week?

_____
_____

What will I do differently?

_____
_____

Thoughts about my daily activities

⊛ _____
⊛ _____
⊛ _____
⊛ _____
⊛ _____

*I am generous*

# New week. *New goals.*

Week Start Date _____

This week's daily habits

- 🕯️ Heart _____
- 🧠 Head _____
- 🧘 Health _____
- 👥 Relationships _____
- 🚀 Mission _____

_____

Goals for this week
_____
_____
_____

What is my 'WHY'
_____
_____

## Monday

I am _____
_____
_____
_____
_____
_____

Today's tasks towards my goal
_____
_____

Today I am GRATEFUL for
_____
_____
_____
_____
_____
_____
_____
_____

Daily Habits Checklist  🕯️ 🧠 🧘 👥 🚀    *I am full of energy*

## Tuesday

I am _____

_____

_____

_____

_____

_____

Today's tasks towards my goal

_____

_____

_____

Daily Habits Checklist  ⊚ ⊚ ⊚ ⊚ ⊚

Today I am GRATEFUL for

_____

_____

_____

_____

_____

_____

_____

_____

_____

*I am sensational*

---

## Wednesday

I am _____

_____

_____

_____

_____

_____

_____

Today's tasks towards my goal

_____

_____

_____

Daily Habits Checklist  ⊚ ⊚ ⊚ ⊚ ⊚

Today I am GRATEFUL for

_____

_____

_____

_____

_____

_____

_____

_____

_____

*I am fortunate*

## Thursday

I am _____

_____

_____

_____

_____

_____

Today's tasks towards my goal

_____

_____

_____

Daily Habits Checklist  ⊙ ⊙ ⊙ ⊙ ⊙

Today I am GRATEFUL for
_____

_____

_____

_____

_____

_____

_____

_____

_____

*I am proud*

---

## Friday

I am _____

_____

_____

_____

_____

_____

Today's tasks towards my goal

_____

_____

_____

Daily Habits Checklist  ⊙ ⊙ ⊙ ⊙ ⊙

Today I am GRATEFUL for
_____

*Happiness is a direction - not a place.*

_____

_____

_____

_____

_____

_____

_____

*I am resilient*

# Saturday

I am _____

_____
_____
_____
_____
_____

Today's tasks towards my goal

_____
_____

Daily Habits Checklist  ⊛ ⊛ ⊛ ⊛ ⊛

Today I am GRATEFUL for

_____
_____
_____
_____
_____
_____
_____
_____
_____

*I am independent*

---

# Sunday Reflection

I am GRATEFUL for

_____
_____

What was successful about this week?

_____
_____

What will I do differently?

_____
_____
_____

Thoughts about my daily activities

⊛ _____
⊛ _____
⊛ _____
⊛ _____
⊛ _____

*I am enough*

## Stay in Touch

 fb.com/kathyshanks

 uplevelyourlife

 uplevel-your-life.com

**Join our FB Community**
fb.com/groups/uplevelmembers

www.ingramcontent.com/pod-product-compliance
Lightning Source LLC
Chambersburg PA
CBHW040800150426
4281ICB00056B/1100